Spanish

BUSINESS
PHRASE BOOK

WITH BUSINESS DICTIONARIES
BY P.H. COLLIN

Bob M...

520 88

Easy to us...

Handy thematic colour coding

Quick reference pronunciation guide — opposite page

Country factfiles – inside back cover

Question and multiple response indicators throughout

How best to use this Phrase Book

This business phrase book has been designed to provide the handiest reference source to suit your business needs — whether you're on a trip to Spain or Latin America, entertaining a Spanish-speaking visitor, or corresponding by telephone, fax or letter with a Spanish-speaking business partner.

- Consult the **Contents** pages (3-4) to locate the section you need. Separate, descriptive contents lists are included at the beginning of each chapter, to help you find your way around.

- Your fastest look-up is via the **English-Spanish dictionary** (pp. 125-160), which contains over 2,500 essential business terms. For help in translating Spanish documents, use the **Spanish-English dictionary** (pp.161-191).

- For more technical terminology, consult **Industries and professions** (pp. 97-124). This section contains specific terms for use in 12 major business fields.

- Practical guidelines and the essential phrases for telephoning and introducing yourself and your company are provided in the section on **Making contact** (pp. 5-32).

- For more complex business situations, consult **Communication skills** (pp. 33-64). Sequenced phrases provide a progressive framework for developing meetings and negotiations successfully.

- For day-to-day business transactions, **Company departments** (pp. 65-96) provides the essential terms and model phrases for dealing effectively with your Spanish-speaking counterpart.

Note: where applicable, feminine forms appear in parentheses, e.g. **ocupado(-a)**: feminine adjective *ocupada*. With nouns, the appropriate feminine article should be substituted, e.g. **el director(a)**: feminine noun *la directora*.

Where usage differs between Spain and Spanish-speaking America, the alternative for the latter appears in square brackets [ ].

CONTENTS

Acknowledgements

This material was developed in association with Nick Brieger and Jeremy Comfort of York Associates, and JOHN GREEN TEFL TAPES; business dictionaries were compiled by Peter Collin Publishing Ltd; our thanks also to Able Translations Ltd – a division of Berlitz International Inc. and Oxford Brookes Language Services for their help in the preparation of this book.

Making Contact

BUSINESS COMMUNICATION

On the Telephone

answering machine	el contestador automático
code	el código
conference call	la conversación telefónica a varias bandas
direct line	la línea directa
engaged/busy	comunicando(-a)/ocupado(-a)
extension	la extensión
get through	pasar con
switchboard	la centralita
telephone (n)/(v)	el teléfono/llamar por teléfono [telefonear]
telephone directory	el listín telefónico [la guía telefónica]

Identifying yourself

● Hello.	● ¿Dígame? Al habla. [¿Hola/Pronto?]
● ... Co./Inc. here. Can I help you?	● ... S.A. ¿Dígame?
▶ Good morning/afternoon.	▶ Buenos días/Buenas tardes.
▶ My name is ...	▶ Soy ...
▶ This is ... here.	▶ Le llama ...

Asking to speak to someone

Could I speak to ... please?	¿Podría hablar con ..., por favor?

INTRODUCTIONS, see page 23

Could you put me through to ... please?	¿Podría ponerme [comunicarme] con ..., por favor?
Can I have extension 351 please?	Póngame [Comuníqueme] con la extensión 351, por favor.
Could I speak to someone who deals with ...?	¿Podría hablar con el encargado de ...?
▶ Who's calling?	▶ ¿Me dice su nombre, por favor?
▶ Could you tell me what it's about?	▶ ¿Le importa decirme de qué se trata?
▶ Can I help you?	▶ ¿En qué puedo ayudarle?
▶ Who would you like to speak to?	▶ ¿Con quién quiere hablar?
▶ Speaking.	▶ Sí, soy yo.

Giving the reason for the call

It's in connection with ...	Es en relación con ...
It's about ...	Se trata de ...
I'm calling about ...	Llamo en relación a ...
I'm phoning to tell you ...	Llamo para decirle que ...
The reason I'm calling is ...	La razón de mi llamada es ...

Making excuses

I'm afraid _____ is ...	Lo siento _____ ...
not available.	no puede ponerse [atenderle].
in a meeting.	está en una reunión.
with a customer at the moment.	está reunido(-a)/con un cliente (una clienta) en este momento.
I'm sorry but _____ ...	Lo siento pero _____ ...
is on holiday/vacation.	está de vacaciones.
is not in the office.	no está en la oficina.
is on the other line at present.	está hablando por la otra línea.
is no longer with the company.	ya no trabaja con nosotros.
I'm afraid his line's engaged/busy.	Lo siento, está comunicando [su línea está ocupada].
Do you want to hold?	¿Desea esperar?
Can I pass you to his/her ...	¿Quiere hablar con su ...?
assistant/colleague/replacement	ayudante(-a)/compañero(-a)/suplente

Taking a message

Would you like to leave a message?	¿Quiere dejarle algún mensaje?

INTRODUCING YOUR COMPANY, see pages 28 & 45

May I take a message?	¿Quiere que le dé algún mensaje?
Can I take your name and number?	¿Le importa darme su nombre y número de teléfono?
Can I get him to call you back?	¿Le digo que le llame más tarde?
● Please leave a message after the tone.	● Habla después del pitido.

Leaving a message

Could you give him a message?	¿Le importaría dejarle un mensaje?
Could you ask her to call me back? The number is ...	Dígale que me llame más tarde. El número de teléfono es ...
Could you tell her I'll call back later?	Dígale que le llamaré más tarde.

Showing you understand

I see.	Ya veo.
I understand.	Entiendo.
Right/Fine/Okay.	Bien/Muy bien/Vale.

Communication problems

Could you repeat that?	¿Le importa repetírmelo?
I'm sorry, I didn't catch your name.	Perdón, no he entendido su nombre.
Could you speak a little slower/louder?	¿Le importaría hablar un poco más despacio/alto?
It's a very bad line. I'll call you back.	Hay muchas interferencias. Voy a llamarle otra vez.
Could you spell that please?	¿Le importaría deletreármelo?
Let me just repeat that: ...	Se lo repito: ...

Ending the call

Thanks very much for your help.	Muchas gracias por su ayuda.
I'm grateful for your assistance.	Le agradezco su ayuda.
I look forward ...	Espero ...
to seeing you soon.	verle pronto.
hearing from you.	sus noticias.
See you soon.	Hasta pronto.
Good-bye/Bye.	Adiós./Hasta luego.
Thanks for calling.	Gracias por llamar/su llamada.

TELEPHONE NUMBERS, see page 18

CORRESPONDENCE

Commercial correspondence in Spanish is generally fairly formal.
Clear, simple sentences are preferred, though, to convoluted structures.

The preliminaries

The typical layout for a letter is:

Vinos del Prado S.A. *Plaza de la villa, 513, Córdoba*

Señores (de) Worldwines   Córdoba, 18 de mai de 199-
14 Barrel Lane
London MW3 0PD

Su ref. Factura 10587
Nuestra ref. ST/154

If there is no letterhead, the sender's address will appear in the upper
right corner. For a fax, the essential details are:

Vinos Pérez S.A.   *Mesaje de Fax*

A: Worldwines
A la atención de: Peter Brown
Fax: +44 01234 683445
De/Trasmisor: Pablo Pérez
Fax: +34 01987 654321
Páginas: 1
Fecha: 23 de marzo de 199_

The greeting

Dear Sir *(name unknown)*	**Muy Señor mio: [Estimado señor:]**
Dear Mr. Ríos *(name known)*	**Estimado Señor/Sr. Ríos:**
Dear Mrs. Marcos *(name known)*	**Estimado Señorita/Sra. Marcos:**
Dear Sir(s) *(formal, to a firm)*	**Muy señor(es) nuestro(s):**
	[Estimado(s) señor(es):]
Dear Director *(important position)*	**Señor Director:**
Dear Friend *(fairly informal)*	**Mi estimado amigo:**

The start

With reference to ...	**Con referencia con ...**
Thank you for your letter of _____ (*date*), ...	**Gracias por su carta del día ...**
I have received your letter of _____ (*date*), ...	**He recibido su carta del día ...**
asking if/about ...	**preguntando si/sobre ...**
concerning ...	**relativa a ...**
enclosing ...	**adjuntando ...**
in which you asked ...	**en la que me pregunta ...**

Explaining the purpose

We are writing to inquire about/whether ...	**Le escribimos para consultarles sobre/si ...**
I am writing in connection with ...	**Escribo en relación con ...**
In response to ...	**Para dar respuesta a ...**
With reference to ...	**A propósito de ...**
With regard to ...	**Con respecto a ...**

Requesting

We would be very grateful if you could ...	**Le estaríamos muy agradecidos si pudiera ...**
I would be much obliged if you could ...	**Le agradeceríamos que ...**
We would appreciate it if you could ...	**Le estaríamos muy reconocidos si pudiera ...**
Please could you ... (*informal*)	**¿No podría ...?**

Giving information or replying to a request for information

Positive

Please find enclosed ...	**Adjunto le enviamos ...**
We are happy to enclose ...	**Nos complace adjuntarle ...**
We wish to inform you that ...	**Deseamos informarle de que ...**
We are pleased to inform you that ...	**Tenemos el placer de comunicarle que ...**

Negative

We regret to inform you that ...	**Lamentamos comunicarle que ...**
We are sorry to tell you that ...	**Sentimos tener que decirle que ...**

Thanking

I am much obliged to you for sending me ...	**Le estoy muy agradecido(-a) por enviarme ...**
I am grateful to you for ...	**Le agradezco que ...**
We are much obliged to you for	**Le estamos muy agradecidos(-as) por ...**
Thank you for ... *(informal)*	**Muchas gracias por ...**

Apologizing

We were extremely sorry to hear about the problem.	**Nos disgusta profundamente que se haya producido este problema.**
We regret that this problem has happened.	**Lamentamos que se haya producido este problema.**
We apologise for ...	**Pedimos disculpas por ...**

Linking ideas

The following linking words show the relationship between your sentences and can make your letter easier to read.

cause	
therefore	**por esta razón**
so/consequently	**por ello/en consecuencia**
comparison	
similarly/in the same way	**igualmente/de la misma forma**
that is/namely	**esto es/a saber**
contrast	
however/nevertheless	**sin embargo/no obstante**
addition	
in addition/also/too	**además/y también/también**
equivalence	
in other words/that means	**en otras palabras/esto significa que**
likewise	**asimismo**
inclusion	
for example/e.g.	**por ejemplo/p.ej.**
such as/as follows	**tal como/de la siguiente forma**

highlight
in particular/especially/mainly — **en particular/especialmente/principalmente**

generalization
usually/normally/as a rule — **generalmente/normalmente/como norma**

stating the obvious
obviously/naturally/of course — **obviamente/naturalmente/por supuesto**

summary
in summary/to sum up — **en resumen/en resumidas cuentas/en general**

overall/in brief — **en pocas/breves palabras/en breve**

conclusion
in conclusion/finally — **en conclusión/finalmente**
lastly — **en última instancia**

The closing

Please don't hesitate to contact if you need any further information. — **Por favor, si necesita más información no dude en ponerse en contacto con nosotros.**

We look forward to meeting you/hearing from you. — **Esperamos verle pronto/sus (gratas) noticias.**

We look forward to receiving your proposal/order/reply. — **En espera de su propuesta/pedido/respuesta.**

The farewell

Yours sincerely *(formal)*
(from more than one signatory) — **Le(s) saludan atentamente**
(to more than one person) — **Les saluda(n) atentemente**

Yours sincerely *(less formal)* — **Reciba un atento saludo**
With best wishes — **Con los mejores deseos**
With best regards — **Un cordial saludo**
All the best — **Un afectuaso saludo de**
Signed — **Firmado/Fdo.**

The enclosures

Encl. — **Adjunto/Adj.**

ARRANGING APPOINTMENTS

appointment	la cita
calendar	el calendario
date	la fecha
diary	la agenda
engagement	el compromiso
meeting	la reunión
schedule	el plan
timetable	el horario

Opening

You may remember, ... we met at ...	Recuerde que ... nos conocimos en ...
... suggested I contact you.	... me sugirió que le llamara.
I feel we should get together.	Creo que deberíamos vernos.
Mr/Mrs .... said he/she would like to talk about ...	El Señor/La Señora ... dijo que le gustaría hablar sobre ...
I'd like to tell you about ...	Me gustaría hablarle de ...
I'd like to arrange a meeting.	Me gustaría concertar una cita.
Let's fix a date.	Vamos a fijar una fecha.
Could we meet?	¿Podríamos vernos?

● Could you tell me what it's about?   ● ¿Le importa decirme de qué se trata?

● Why do want to see Mr/Mrs Ramírez?   ● ¿Para qué quiere ver al Señor/ a la Señora Ramírez?

▶ I'd like to discuss ...   ▶ Me gustaría hablar de ...

▶ We need to talk about ...   ▶ Tenemos que hablar de ...

Arranging a time

Could you manage next week?	¿Le viene bien la próxima semana/la semana que viene?
What about Friday afternoon?	¿Qué tal el viernes por la tarde?
Would Monday suit you?	¿El lunes le viene bien?
Shall we say 2 o'clock?	¿A las 2?

▶ I'm afraid I can't manage Friday.   ▶ Me temo que el viernes no puede ser.

▶ Next week is out.   ▶ La semana que viene está fuera.

▶ Can you make the following week?   ▶ ¿Podría ser la semana siguiente?

▶ Tuesday would suit me better.   ▶ El martes me vendría mejor

▶ 4 o'clock would be fine.   ▶ A las 4 sería perfecto.

DATES, see page 15/TIME, see page 16

Duration

It'll have to be short. I've got another meeting at 5.	**Tendrá que ser breve. Tengo otra reunión a las 5.**
It won't take more than an hour.	**No será/llevará más de una hora.**

Place

Where do you suggest?	**¿Dónde le parece que nos veamos?**
I'll come to your office.	**Iré a su oficina.**
Shall we meet in my office?	**¿Puede venir a mi oficina?/¿Nos vemos en mi oficina?**

Directions

Can you give me some directions?	**¿Puede decirme cómo llegar?**
Will you be coming by car?	**¿Va a venir en coche?**
I would take a taxi from the airport.	**Yo cogería [tomaría] un taxi en el aeropuerto.**
I'll fax you a map.	**Le enviaré un plano por fax.**
Just ask for me at the reception desk	**Pregunte por mí en la recepción.**
My office is on the fifth floor (*US* sixth floor).	**Mi oficina está en quinta planta.**

Ending

Let me just confirm that. Friday 24th, 3:30 at your office.	**Deje que lo confirme. El viernes 24 a las 3:30 en su oficina.**
I look forward to seeing you then.	**Nos veremos entonces.**
See you next Friday.	**Le veré el viernes.**

En route

Where can I get a taxi?	**¿Dónde puedo coger [tomar] un taxi?**
Could you take me to …?	**¿Puede llevarme a …?**
Could you tell me how to get to …?	**¿Puede decirme cómo llegar a …?**
Where can I park?	**¿Dónde puedo aparcar [estacionar]?**
▶ Straight ahead.	▶ **Todo recto [derecho].**
▶ Turn left/right.	▶ **Gire a la izquierda/derecha.**
▶ You'll see it on your right/left.	▶ **Lo verá a su derecha/izquierda.**

TRAVELLING AROUND, see page 19

Arriving

My name's ...	Soy ...
I've got an appointment with ...	Estoy citado(-a) con .../Tengo una cita con ...
▶ Could I see your identity card?	▶ ¿Me permite su carné de identidad [documentación]?
▶ Please take a seat.	▶ Siéntese, por favor.
▶ Mr/Mrs ... will see you now.	▶ El Señor/La Señora ... le atenderá ahora mismo.
▶ She'll be with you shortly.	▶ Le atenderá en unos minutos.

Cancelling an appointment

Unfortunately, I'll have to cancel our meeting on ...	Desgraciadamente tengo que cancelar nuestra reunión del ...
I'll be unable to make the meeting.	Me será imposible asistir a la reunión.
● Can we fix a new time? How about ...?	● ¿Podemos concertar una nueva cita? ¿Le parece bien el ...?
▶ I'll check.	▶ Lo comprobaré.
▶ I'm afraid that's not possible.	▶ Me temo que es imposible.

Months

January	enero
February	febrero
March	marzo
April	abril
May	mayo
June	junio
July	julio
August	agosto
September	septiembre
October	octubre
November	noviembre
December	diciembre

Seasons

spring	la primavera
summer	el verano
in autumn/the fall	en otoño *m*
during winter	durante el invierno

Date

● What's the date today?	● ¿Qué fecha es?
▶ It's April 23rd.	▶ Es el veintitrés de abril.

January 1st	uno de enero
on September 7	el siete de septiembre
in May	en mayo
from June to August	de junio a agosto
the beginning of June	a principios de junio
the middle of July	a mediados de julio
the end of August	a finales de agosto

Years

1996	mil novecientos noventa y seis
1998	mil novecientos noventa y ocho
2001	dos mil uno
in 2010	en dos mil diez

Days

Monday	lunes
Tuesday	martes
Wednesday	miércoles
Thursday	jueves
Friday	viernes
Saturday	sábado
Sunday	domingo

today	hoy
tomorrow	mañana
the day after tomorrow	pasado mañana
yesterday	ayer
the day before yesterday	anteayer
this Wednesday	este miércoles
next Friday	el próximo viernes
a week on from Tuesday	el martes de la semana que viene
by Thursday	el jueves a más tardar
on Saturday	el sábado
on Mondays/every Monday	los lunes/todos los lunes
in 5 days' time	dentro de cinco días
last/next month	el mes pasado/que viene
for 3 days	durante tres días

NUMBERS, see page 17

Times of day

early morning	**a primera hora de la mañana**
morning	**por la mañana**
midday	**a mediodía**
lunchtime	**a la hora de comer**
before lunch	**antes de comer**
after lunch	**después de comer**
afternoon	**por la tarde**
late afternoon	**a última hora de la tarde**
evening	**por la noche**

Time

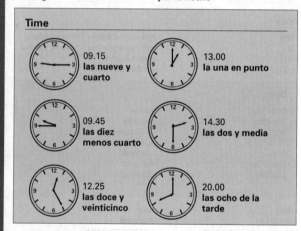

09.15
las nueve y cuarto

13.00
la una en punto

09.45
las diez menos cuarto

14.30
las dos y media

12.25
las doce y veinticinco

20.00
las ocho de la tarde

It's one/two o'clock. — **Es la una/Son las dos.**

- What time does it start/end? — **¿A qué hora empieza/termina?**
  - ▸ at 9 a.m. — ▸ **a las nueve de la mañana**
  - ▸ by 3 o'clock — ▸ **parsa las tres**
- How long will it last? — **¿Cuánto durará?**
  - ▸ 10 minutes — ▸ **diez minutos**
  - ▸ ¾ of an hour — ▸ **tres cuartos de hora**

from ... up to ... — **desde ... hasta ...**

about ... — **sobre/a eso de ...**

... exactly — **... exactamente**

... at the latest — **... como muy tarde [a más tardar]**

Numbers

0	cero	50	cincuenta
1	un/uno	60	sesenta
2	dos	70	setenta
3	tres	80	ochenta
4	cuatro	90	noventa
5	cinco	100	cien/ciento
6	seis	110	ciento diez
7	siete	200	doscientos(-as)
8	ocho	300	trescientos(-as)
9	nueve	400	cuatrocientos(-as)
10	diez	500	quinientos(-as)
11	once	600	seiscientos(-as)
12	doce	700	setecientos(-as)
13	trece	800	ochocientos(-as)
14	catorce	900	novecientos(-as)
15	quince	1000	mil
16	dieciséis	1100	mil cien
17	diecisiete	1200	mil descientos
18	dieciocho	2000	dos mil
19	diecinueve	5000	cinco mil
20	veinte	10.000	diez mil
21	veintiuno	50.000	cincuenta mil
22	veintidós	100.000	cien mil
30	treinta	1.000.000	un millón
40	cuarenta	1.000.000.000	mil millones

Ordinal numbers

first (1st)	**primero(-a) (1º/1ª)**
second (2nd)	**segundo(-a) (2º/2ª)**
third (3rd)	**tercero(-a) (3º/3ª)**
fourth	**cuarto(-a)**
fifth	**quinto(-a)**
sixth	**sexto(-a)**
seventh	**séptimo(-a)**
eighth	**octavo(-a)**
ninth	**noveno(-a)**
tenth	**décimo(-a)**
hundredth	**centésimo(-a)**
millionth	**milionésimo(-a)**

Fractions etc.

a half	**una mitad, un medio**
a quarter	**un cuarto**
one third	**un tercio**
four fifths	**cuatro quintos**
a pair of	**una docena**
a dozen	**un paio**
one per cent	**un por ciento**
3.4	**tres coma cuatro (3,4)**
once/twice/three times	**una vez/dos veces/tres veces**

Telephone numbers

Telephone numbers are usually read in pairs.

34 - 1 - 45-56-78	**treinta y cuatro - uno - cuarenta y cinco - cincuenta y seis - setenta y ocho**

Money

10,523.50 pesetas	**diez mil quinientas veintitrés con cincuenta pesetas (10.523,50 ptas)**
$10 per unit	**diez dólares por unidad**
profits have doubled trebled/halved	**los beneficios se han duplicado triplicado/reducido a la mitad**

Reference numbers

254/DG	**doscientos cincuenta y cuatro barra de ge**
3580-00	**treinta y cinco ochenta raya cero cero**

Measurements

1.2 metres/meters	**un metro, viente centímetras (1,2m)**
500 litres/liters	**quinientos litros**
about 20 stores	**unos veinte almacenes**
in the region of ⅞ths	**alrededor de siete octavos**
between 50 and 60 percent	**entre el cincuenta y el sesenta por ciento**
30-40,000	**de treinta a cuarenta mil**
sales have dropped/risen by 30,000 units	**las ventas han aumentado/ descendido en treinta mil unidades**

TRAVELLING AROUND

Travel by plane

Is there a (connecting) flight to ...?	¿Hay algún vuelo (de conexión) para ...?
When does it leave/take off?	¿A qué hora sale/despega?
When does it arrive/land?	¿A qué hora llega/aterriza?
What time do I have to check in?	¿A qué hora tengo que facturar?

Booking and changing flights

ticket	el billete [el pasaje]
single/one-way	de ida
economy class	de clase turista
business class	de clase preferente
I'd like to book a return/round-trip flight to...	Me gustaría reservar un vuelo de ida y vuelta para ...
I'd like to cancel/change my reservation on flight number ...	Quisiera cancelar mi reserva del vuelo número ...

Travel by train

buffet/restaurant car	la cafetería/el vagón restaurante
couchette/sleeping car	la litera/el coche cama
first-class compartment	el compartimiento de primera clase
platform	la vía, el andén
ticket office	el despacho de billetes [la venta de pasajes]
ticket reservation	la reserva de billetes [de pasajes]
timetable	el horario

Enquiring about rail travel

When is the next train to ...?	¿Cuándo sale el próximo tren para ...?
What's the fare to ...?	¿Cuánto cuesta el billete [pasaje] para ...?
Do I have to change?	¿Tengo que cambiar de tren?
When does it arrive at ...?	¿A qué hora llega el tren a ...?
Which platform does the train leave from/arrive at?	¿De qué anden sale/A qué anden llega el tren?

Buying a ticket

I'd like a single/one-way ticket to ...	Quisiera un billete [pasaje] de ida para ...
return/round trip	de ida y vuelta
first-class	en primera
I'd like to reserve a seat.	Quisiera reservar un billete. [Quisiera reservar un pasaje.]

On the train

Is this the right train to ...?	¿Es éste el tren que va a ...?
Is this seat taken?	¿Está ocupado este asiento?
I think that's my seat.	Creo que éste es mi asiento.

Travel by taxi

Could you get me a taxi?	¿Podría conseguirme un taxi?
Where is the taxi rank/stand?	¿Dónde hay una parada de taxis?
Take me to ...	Lléveme ...
the Trade Fair	al recinto ferial
this address	a esta dirección
Please stop here.	Pare aquí, por favor.
Could you wait for me?	¿Podría esperarme aquí, por favor?
I'll be back in 10 minutes.	Vuelvo en diez minutos.
How much do I owe you?	¿Cuánto le debo?
Keep the change.	Quédese con el cambio.

Travel by car

Car hire/rental

I'd like to hire/rent a car.	Quisiera alquilar un coche.
small	pequeño
medium-sized	mediano
automatic	automático
with air-conditioning	con aire acondicionado
Is mileage included?	¿Va incluido el kilometraje?
I'd like to leave the car in ...	Quisiera dejar el coche en ...
How much is the deposit?	¿Cuánto es la fianza?
I'd like full insurance.	Quisiera un seguro a todo riesgo.

At the petrol/gas station

Could you fill it up, please?	**Lleno, por favor.**
petrol/gasoline	**la gasolina**
regular/premium/unleaded	**normal/súper/sin plomo**

Garage–Breaking down

My car's broken down.	**Mi coche se ha averiado.**
May I use your phone?	**¿Puedo usar su teléfono?**
My car won't start.	**Mi coche no arranca.**
The battery is dead.	**Me he quedado sin batería.**
I've run out of petrol.	**Me he quedado sin gasolina.**
I've got a flat tyre/tire.	**Tengo un neumático bajo.**
There's something wrong with the ...	**Algo va mal con ...**
Please check the ...	**Compruebe, por favor ...**
battery	**la batería**
brakes	**los frenos**
spare tyre/tire	**la rueda de repuesto**
tyre/tire pressure	**la presión**

Accidents

Where's the nearest ...?	**¿Dónde está ... más cercano?**
telephone/garage	**el teléfono/el taller**
Could you call an ambulance?	**¿Podría llamar una ambulancia?**
Here's my driving licence/ driver's license.	**Aquí tiene mi permiso de conducir.**
What's you name and address?	**¿Cuál es su nombre y dirección?**
What's your insurance company.	**¿Cuál es su compañía de seguros?**

Directions

Go straight ahead.	**Siga todo recto. [Siga derecho.]**
It's on the left/right.	**Está a la izquierda/derecha.**
opposite/behind ...	**en frente/detrás ...**
next to/after ...	**junto a/después de ...**
Turn left at the ...	**Gire a la izquierda después ...**
next corner	**de la siguiente esquina**
traffic lights	**del semáforo**
Take the A3.	**Coja [Tome] la A3.**
You have to go back to ...	**Tiene que dar la vuelta y ...**

Accommodation

Booking a room

I'd like a single room for two nights.	Quisiera una habitación individual para dos noches.
From ... to ...	Desde ... hasta ...
single room	habitación individual
double room	habitación doble
twin-bedded room	habitación con dos camas
family room	habitación triple
with bath/shower	con baño/ducha
I'd like a room with a shower.	Quisiera una habitación con ducha.
It must be quiet.	Tiene que ser tranquila.
I'll be arriving late.	Llegaré tarde.
How much does it cost?	¿Cuánto cuesta?
Do you accept credit cards?	¿Aceptan tarjetas de crédito?

Registering at a hotel

● My name's ...	● Mi nombre es ...
● I've got a reservation for two nights.	● Tengo una reserva para dos noches.
▶ Could you fill in this form?	▶ ¿Le importa rellenar este formulario?
▶ How will you be paying?	▶ ¿Cómo va a pagar?
▶ May I see your credit card?	▶ ¿Puedo ver su tarjeta de crédito?

Complaining

Could I have a quieter room?	¿Podría conseguirme una habitación más tranquila?
My room's too small/noisy.	Mi habitación es demasiado pequeña/ruidosa.

Checking out

May I have the bill please?	¿Me prepara la cuenta, por favor?
I'm leaving early in the morning so could you have the bill ready?	Me iré a primera hora de la mañana. ¿Podría tenerme la cuenta preparada?
There's a mistake in this bill.	Hay un error en la cuenta.
Can you order a taxi please?	¿Podría pedirme un taxi?

DATES, see page 15

INTRODUCTIONS

Shake hands on introduction; business cards are usually exchanged at the end of the meeting.

When referring to people, as in introductions, the relevant article precedes their title, e.g. **el Señor Ríos**, **la Señora Carlos**, **el Doctor Gómez.** Note that this does not apply to the use of courtesy titles **Don** and **Doña**, e.g. **Don Fernando Pérez, Doña María.**

Greetings

Hello.	**Hola.**
Good morning/afternoon.	**Buenos días/Buenas tardes.**
Good evening.	**Buenas noches.**
How do you do?	**¿Cómo está?**
Pleased to meet you.	**Mucho gusto./Encantado(-a) de conocerle.**

Introducing yourself

My name's ...	**Me llamo ...**
I'm ...	**Soy ...**
Please call me ...	**Llámeme ...**
Everybody calls me ...	**Todo el mundo/Todos me llaman ...**

Responding

How do you do? I'm ...	**¿Cómo está? Soy .../Me llamo ...**
Pleased to meet you too. My name's ...	**Encantado(-a) de conocerle. Yo soy .../Me llamo ...**
Nice to meet you too.	**El gusto es mío.**

Introducing others

Peter, this is ...	**Peter, te presento a ...**
May I introduce you to ...	**Le presento a ...**
Have you two met? This is ...	**¿Se conocen? Le presento a ...**

Everyday greetings

● How are you?	● **¿Cómo está?**
▶ Fine, and you?	▶ **Muy bien, ¿y usted?**
▶ Not so bad.	▶ **Como siempre/Bien, bien.**
▶ Could be worse.	▶ **No mal del todo.**

MAKING CONTACT

Presenting your job

- What do you do?
- What line are you in?
- I'm ...
  a secretary
  an engineer
  an accountant

- I work in ...
  an insurance company
  a school

- I work for ...
  IBM/the local newspaper
  a pharmaceutical company

- I'm on the ... side.
  technical/commercial
  administrative

- I'm in ...
  marketing
  sales/finance

- I'm self-employed/
  unemployed/retired

- ¿A qué se dedica?
- ¿Cuál es su trabajo?
- Soy ...
  secretario(-a)
  ingeniero(-a)
  contable [contador(a)]

- Trabajo en ...
  una empresa de seguros
  un colegio

- Trabajo para ...
  IBM/el periódico local
  una empresa farmacéutica

- Trabajo para la parte ...
  técnica/comercial
  administrativa

- Estoy en ...
  marketing
  ventas/finanzas

- Soy autónomo(-a) [Trabajo por
  cuenta propia]/Estoy en el paro
  [Estoy desempleado(-a)]/Estoy
  jubilado(-a)

Origins

- Where do you come from?
- Where do you live?

● ¿De dónde es?	
● ¿Dónde vive?	

- I come from ... *I'm ...*

		Soy de ...	Soy ...
Argentina	*Argentinian*	Argentina	*argentino(-a)*
Australia	*Australian*	Australia	*australiano (-a)*
Britain	*British*	Gran Bretaña	*británico(-a)*
Canada	*Canadian*	Canadá	*canadiense*
England	*English*	Inglaterra	*inglés(-esa)*
Ireland	*Irish*	Irlanda	*irlandés(-esa)*
Mexico	*Mexican*	Méjico	*mejicano(-a)*
		[México]	*[mexicano(-a)]*
Scotland	*Scottish*	Escocia	*escocés(-esa)*
Spain	*Spanish*	España	*español(a)*
United States	*American*	los Estados	*estadounidense*
		Unidos	
Wales	*Welsh*	Gales	*galés(-esa)*

Introductions

COMPANY POSITIONS, see page 28

Socializing

After-hours socializing is usually conducted in a restaurant; it is not common to be invited to someone's house. Punctuality is appreciated, though arriving a few minutes late is acceptable.

Arriving

● How was your trip?	● ¿Qué tal el viaje?
● How was the journey?	● ¿Ha tenido un buen viaje?
▶ Not bad.	▶ No ha estado mal.
▶ No problems.	▶ Sin problemas.
▶ Rather long.	▶ Bastante largo.
● When did you arrive?	● ¿Cuándo ha llegado?
● When did you get in?	● ¿Cuándo ha llegado?
● Did you ...	● ¿Ha venido en ...?
take the train/fly?	tren/avión
come by car/drive?	coche
▶ I came by car/I drove.	▶ He venido en coche.
▶ I took the last flight.	▶ Cogí [Tomé] el último vuelo.

Leaving

● I'm leaving tomorrow.	● Me voy mañana.
▶ What time does your plane leave?	▶ ¿A qué hora sale su avión?
▶ When do you have to check in?	▶ ¿A qué hora tiene que facturar su equipaje?

Could you book a taxi for me?	¿Puede pedirme un taxi?
I need a taxi to take me to the airport.	Necesito que un taxi me lleve al aeropuerto.
How long do you think it will take?	¿Cuánto cree que tardará?

Accommodation

● How's your hotel?	● ¿Está bien el hotel?
▶ Yes, it's fine.	▶ Sí, todo está bien.
▶ It's OK.	▶ Es perfecto.
▶ It's a bit noisy.	▶ Es un poco ruidoso.

Weather

What a lovely day!	¡Qué día tan bonito!
What awful weather!	¡Qué tiempo tan desagradable!

TRAVELLING AROUND, see page 19/ACCOMMODATION, see page 22

Introductions

- What was the weather like when you left?
- Much the same as here.
- Very sunny.
- Dreadful.
- Lovely and warm.
- Cold for the time of year.

- ¿Qué tiempo hacía al salir/cu? cuando salió?
- Muy parecido al de aquí.
- Muy soleado.
- Desagradable.
- Muy agradable.
- Un poco frío para este tiempo.

Family

- Are you married?
- Yes, my wife is ...
- My husband is ...
- No, I'm single.
  I'm divorced.

- ¿Está casado(-a)?
- Sí, mi mujer es ...
- Mi marido es ...
- No, estoy soltero(-a).
  Estoy divorciado(-a).

- Have you got any children?
- Yes, two boys and a girl.
  one daughter/three sons

- ¿Tienes niños?
- Sí, dos niños y una niña.
  una hija/tres hijos

- How old are they?
- They're ten and twelve.
- The oldest/youngest is ...
- Oh, they've left home.

- ¿Cuántos años tienen?
- Tienen diez y doce años.
- El/La mayor/menor tiene ...
- Son mayores, ya no viven en casa.

Interests

- What do you do at/on the weekends?
- Are you interested in sports?
- Do you play any sports?
- I play football/golf/rugby/ squash/tennis.
- I don't play but I watch ...
- I go ...
  fishing/swimming/walking

- ¿Qué suele hacer los fines de semana?
- ¿Le gustan los deportes?
- ¿Practica algún deporte?
- Juego al fútbol/golf/rugby/ squash/tenis.
- No juego pero me gusta ver ...
- Suelo ir ....
  a pescar/a nadar/a pasear

Invitations

- Would you like to come to/for dinner?
- I'd like that very much.
- I'd love to but ...
- I'm afraid I can't.
- I've got another engagement.

- ¿Le gustaría venir a cenar?

- Estaría encantado(-a).
- Me gustaría pero ...
- lo siento pero no puedo.
- Tengo otro compromiso.

- Could you manage next Tuesday?
- ¿Podría ser el próximo martes?

▶ Tuesday would be fine.
▶ El martes sería perfecto.

- How about a drink after work?
- ¿Qué tal una copa después del trabajo?

▶ Good idea.
▶ ¡Buena idea!

▶ I'd love to.
▶ Me encantaría.

- Let me buy you a drink.
- Permítame invitarle a una copa.

▶ That's very kind of you.
▶ Muy amable de su parte.

Dining out

Arriving & ordering

We've booked a table for four. **Tenemos una mesa reservada para cuatro personas.**

Could we sit by the window, please? **¿Podríamos sentarnos cerca de la ventana, por favor?**

Are you having a starter/dessert? **¿Desean tomar un aperitivo/un postre?**

I'd recommend the fish. **Les recomiendo pescado.**

What are you going to have? **¿Qué van a tomar?**

I think I'll have the beef. **Creo que tomaré [comeré] carne.**

Could you tell me what ... is? **¿Le importa decirme qué es ...?**

Commenting

The fish is delicious. **El pescado está delicioso.**

Are you enjoying the beef? **¿Les gusta la carne?**

Thank you for a lovely meal. **Gracias por esta estupenda comida.**

Paying

Could I have the bill? **¿Puede hacerme la cuenta, por favor?**

Do you accept ... card? **¿Aceptan tarjeta ...?**

Is the service included? **¿Está incluido el servicio?**

Saying good-bye

I'm afraid we must go now. **Creo que debemos irnos.**

I look forward to seeing you again next year. **Espero verle el año que viene.**

Good-bye/See you soon. **Adiós/Hasta la vista.**

Introducing the company

Sectors

Heavy Industry	la industria pesada
(Light) Manufacturing	la fabricación
Services	los servicios

Types of company

company	la empresa
firm	la firma
partnership	la sociedad
limited company	la sociedad limitada (S.L.)
public limited company/ corporation	la sociedad anónima (S.A.)
state company	la empresa pública
private company	la empresa privada

Parts of company

Head Office/Headquarters	la oficina principal, la sede central
Parent company	la compañía principal
Holding company	el grupo empresarial, el hólding
Subsidiary	la filial
Business Unit	la unidad de gestión
Branch	la sucursal
Sales Office	el punto de venta
Division	la división
Department	el departamento
Section	la sección

Position in a company

Chairman	el presidente(-a)
Managing Director/CEO/ President	el consejero(-a) delegado(-a) [el director(a) ejecutivo(-a)]
Vice President	el vicepresidente(-a)
Director	el director(a)
Manager	el/la gerente
Supervisor	el supervisor(a)
Assistant	el adjunto
Shop floor worker	el empleado(-a) de taller
Office staff	el empleado(-a) administrativo(-a)

PERSONNEL DEPARTMENT, see page 86

People in a company

headcount	la plantilla
staff	la plantilla
personnel	el personal
management	la dirección
workers	los trabajadores

People around the company

suppliers	los proveedores
customers	los clientes
clients	los clientes
agents	los representantes
distributors	los distribuidores
dealers	los agentes, los representantes

Location

We're based in ...	Nuestras oficinas están en ...
Our head office is located in ...	Nuestra oficina central está en ...
We have branches throughout the world.	Tenemos sucursales por todo el mundo.

Activity

We're in the telecommunications field.	Estamos en el campo de las telecomunicaciones.
We're a leading company in ...	Somos una empresa líder en ...
There are three major business units.	Tenemos tres unidades principales de gestión.

Size

There are four partners in the firm.	La empresa tiene cuatro socios.
We employ 20,000 people.	Empleamos a 20.000 personas.
We have 20,000 employees.	Tenemos 20.000 empleados.
Our latest headcount is 20,000.	Nuestra plantilla actual es de 20.000 trabajadores.
We have an annual turnover/ annual sales of $250 million.	Tenemos una facturación de 250 millones de dólares.
Annual profits are in the region of $25 million.	Nuestros beneficios anuales son del orden de los 25 millones de dólares.

Career development

I started as a foreman on the shop floor.	**Comencé como jefe(-a) de taller.**
I got promoted to plant manager.	**Ascendí a director(a) de fábrica.**
I was recently appointed Production Director.	**Recientemente fui nombrado(-a) director(a) de producción.**
I'm due to retire next year.	**Me jubilaré el año que viene.**
I've stayed with the same company.	**He estado en la misma empresa.**
I've worked for ... since 1988/ for 20 years.	**He trabajado para ... desde 1988/ durante 20 años.**
I joined the company 20 years ago.	**Entré en la empresa hace 20 años.**
I've changed jobs often.	**He cambiado de trabajo con mucha frecuencia.**

Company history

Starting

The company was founded in 1884.	**La empresa fue fundada en 1884.**
We set up the company in 1982.	**Constituimos la empresa en 1982.**
The company was first registered in 1982.	**La empresa se inscribió en el registro en 1982.**
We went public 2 years ago.	**Empezamos a cotizar en bolsa hace 2 años.**

Take-overs and mergers

acquisition	**la adquisición**
affiliation	**la afiliación**
consortium	**el consorcio**
merger	**la fusión**
take over (v)	**absorber**
There was a takeover bid.	**Se produjo una oferta pública de adquisición.**
We resisted the bid.	**Resistimos la oferta pública de adquisición.**
We welcomed the bid.	**Aceptamos la oferta pública de adquisición.**
We were taken over by Blaskins.	**Fuimos absorbidos por Blaskins.**
Later we merged with ...	**Después nos fusionamos con ...**

NUMBERS, see page 17/DATES, see page 15

Introducing the product

product line	**la línea de productos**
product features	**las características del producto**
product benefits	**los beneficios del producto**
product advantages	**las ventajas del producto**
Our main product is …	**Nuestro principal producto es …**
We have two major product lines: …	**Tenemos dos líneas de productos principales: …**
It is designed to …	**Está diseñado(-a) para …**
Its main application is in the … industry.	**Su principal aplicación es para el sector …**

Life & service

after sales/customer service	**el servicio de postventa**
maintenance	**el mantenimiento**
repairs	**las reparaciones**
replacement	**el repuesto**
It will last at least ten years.	**Durará un mínimo de diez años.**
It should be regularly serviced.	**Deberá revisarlo periódicamente.**
We have a 24-hour help desk.	**Tenemos un servicio de atención las 24 horas del día.**
Any repairs will be carried out on site.	**Cualquier reparación se realizará a domicilio.**

Delivery

You can expect delivery within 2 weeks.	**Puede esperar la entrega en un plazo de 2 semanas.**
The earliest delivery will be next month.	**La próxima entrega será el mes que viene.**
The delivery may be delayed by 24 hours.	**La entrega puede retrasarse 24 horas.**

Price

low/cheap	**bajo(-a) barato(-a)**
medium/reasonable	**medio(-a)/razonable**
high/expensive	**alto(-a)/caro(-a)**
The product is reasonably-priced.	**El producto tiene un precio razonable.**
We can offer you a 15% discount.	**Podemos ofrecerle un 15% de descuento.**

CUSTOMER SERVICE, see page 66/PRODUCTS, see page 82

Touring the premises

office building	el bloque/edificio de oficinas
plant/factory	la planta/la fábrica/
manufacturing centre/center	el centro de fabricación

Offices

board room	la sala de juntas
canteen / company restaurant	la cafetería/el restaurante de la empresa
corridor	el pasillo
floors	las plantas [los pisos]
lift/elevator	el ascensor
meeting room	la sala de reuniones
open-plan design	el diseño de plan abierto

Office furniture & equipment

desk	el escritorio
fax machine	el fax
filing cabinet	el archivo
PC	el ordenador [la computadora]
photocopier	la fotocopiadora
printer	la impresora
work station	la estación de trabajo

Plant layout

components	los componentes
despatch/dispatch area	los mostradores
factory floor	el taller
machine room	la sala de máquinas
paint shop	el taller de pintura
raw materials	las materias primas

Showing visitors around

I'm pleased to welcome you to …	Me complace darle la bienvenida a …
Welcome to …	Bienvenido(-a) a …
Please come this way.	Por aquí, por favor.
Follow me.	Sígame.
Be careful!	¡Tenga cuidado!
Mind/watch your head!	¡Tenga cuidado con la cabeza!
Over there, you can see …	Allí puede ver …
Are there any questions?	¿Alguna pregunta?

Communication Skills

BUSINESS PRESENTATIONS

Check-list

To help you organize your presentation, it is useful to plan it around the following stages:

1. The introduction	❑	**1. La introducción**	
2. The overview	❑	**2. Los aspectos generales**	
3. The main part	❑	**3. La parte principal**	
4. The summary	❑	**4. El resumen**	
5. The ending	❑	**5. La conclusión**	
6. Questions and answers	❑	**6. Preguntas y respuestas**	

1. The introduction

Good morning/afternoon, ladies and gentlemen.	**Buenos días/Buenas tardes, señoras y señores.**
My name is ...	**Soy ...**
I work for Rossomon as Marketing Director.	**Trabajo para Rossomon como director(a) comercial.**
I am the Personnel Director at Rossomon.	**Soy el director(a) de personal de Rossomon.**
In this talk, I'd like to ... describe the main activities of our company.	**En esta charla, me gustaría ... describir las principales activi- dades de nuestra compañía.**

INTRODUCTIONS, see page 23/COMPANY POSITIONS, see page 28

present our product range.

explain the production processes at our plant.

presentar nuestra gama de productos.

explicar los procesos de producción de nuestra fábrica.

2. The overview

I've divided my talk into 4 main parts.

He dividido mi intervención en 4 partes principales.

My presentation is split into 4 major sections.

Mi presentación está dividida en 4 grandes secciones.

In the description, I aim to cover the 4 key processes.

En la descripción, pretendo cubrir los 4 procesos clave.

Firstly, we'll look at …

En primer lugar, veremos …

Secondly, I'm going to talk about …

En segundo lugar, voy a hablarles de …

After that, I'll tell you about …

A continuación, les hablaré de …

The order of points

First(ly)	Primero (En primer lugar)
Second(ly)	Segundo (En segundo lugar)
Third(ly)	Tercero (En tercer lugar)
Fourth(ly)	Cuarto (En cuarto lugar)
After that	A continuación
Next	Después
Finally	Finalmente

3. The main part

Now let's look at the first point.

Veamos ahora el primer punto.

Now I'd like to start the first part.

Me gustaría empezar la primera parte.

Ending a point

That's all about …

Esto es todo sobre …

That's all I want to say about the first point.

No tengo nada más que decir sobre el primer punto.

NUMBERS, see page 17

That brings me to the end of the first part.	**Con esto termino la primera parte.**

Moving on to the next point

Next let's look at ...	**A continuación veamos ...**
Now I'd like to move on to the next point.	**Ahora me gustaría pasar al siguiente punto.**
So now I'd like to talk about ...	**Ahora me gustaría hablarles de ...**

Visual aids

As you can see on the transparency, ...	**Como pueden ver en la transparencia ...**
You can see the relevant information ...	**Pueden ver la información correspondiente en ...**
on the screen	**la pantalla**
on the monitor	**el monitor**
on the transparency	**la transparencia**
in the illustration	**la ilustración**
in the drawing	**el dibujo**
from the model	**el modelo**
from the plan	**el plano**

The relevant figures are shown ...
Las cifras importantes se muestran ...

on the pie/bar chart	by a solid/broken/dotted line
en el gráfico circular/ el diagrama de barras	**mediante una línea continua/ discontinua/de puntos**

The shaded boxes ...	**Los recuadros sombreados ...**
The unshaded circles ...	**Los círculos no sombreados ...**
The blue triangles ...	**Los triángulos azules ...**
The red rectangles ...	**Los rectángulos rojos ...**
show the major activities.	**muestran las principales actividades.**

COLOURS/COLORS, see page 36

Colours/Colors

black	**negro(-a)**	pink	**rosa**
blue	**azul**	purple	**púrpúra**
brown	**marrón**	red	**rojo(-a)**
green	**verde**	silver	**plateado(-a)**
grey/gray	**gris**	white	**blanco(-a)**
orange	**naranja**	yellow	**amarillo(-a)**

4. The summary

Well, that brings me to the end of my final point.

Con esto doy por terminado el punto final.

That concludes the main part of my talk.

Así concluye la parte principal de mi presentación/intervención.

So now, I'd just like to summarize the main points.

Ahora me gustaría resumir los puntos principales.

In brief, we have looked at …

En resumen, hemos visto …

5. The ending

That's all I have to say for now.

Esto es todo lo que tengo que decir por ahora/el momento.

I hope that …
the presentation has given you all the relevant information for your needs.
the description has provided you with a clear picture of our activities.

**Espero que …
la intervención les haya proporcionado la información que necesitan.
la descripción les haya ofrecido una clara imagen de nuestras actividades.**

6. Questions and answers

If you have any questions, I'll be happy to answer them.

Si tienen alguna pregunta, estaré encantado(-a) de respondérsela.

Your question, please.
Any more questions?

**Sí, dígame.
¿Alguna otra pregunta?**

Does that answer your question?

¿Esto responde a su pregunta?

If there are no more questions, I'd like to thank you for your attention.

Si no hay más preguntas, me gustaría agradecerles su atención.

MEETINGS, CONFERENCES AND TRADE FAIRS

Preparing for the meeting

a chairperson	un presidente(-a)
the participants	los/las participantes
an agenda	el orden del día
a secretary	un secretario(-a)
the minutes	las actas

The agenda

point	el punto
item	el apartado
AOB (any other business)	los ruegos y preguntas
to prepare	preparar
to draft	hacer un borrador de
to circulate	hacer llegar

The time and place

I'd like to call a meeting to discuss ...	Me gustaría convocar una reunión para tratar ...
I'd like to fix a time and place for the meeting.	Me gustaría fijar una fecha y un lugar para la reunión.
Does Monday at ... o'clock suit you?	¿Le viene bien el lunes a la(s) ... en punto?
We are planning to meet in my office/the meeting room.	Pensamos reunirnos en mi oficina/la sala de reuniones.

Preparing the agenda

I've prepared an outline agenda.	He preparado un borrador del orden del día.
Could you look through it, please?	¿Le importaría mirarlo, por favor?
Could you add any points you'd like to discuss?	¿Desea añadir algún punto que le gustaría tratar?
Could I ask you to lead item 2 on staff training?	¿Puedo pedirle que trate el punto 2 sobre formación de personal?
I've finalized the agenda.	Éste es el definitivo orden del día.
You'll receive all the papers tomorrow.	Recibirán todos los documentos mañana.

ARRANGING APPOINTMENTS, see page 12/TIME, see page 16

COMMUNICATION SKILLS

Meetings, conferences and trade fairs

The Chairperson's role

Opening the meeting

Good morning/afternoon, ladies and gentlemen.	**Buenos días/Buenas tardes, señoras y señores.**
If we are all here … let's start/shall we start?	**Si estamos todos, … empecemos/¿podemos empezar?**
First of all I'd like to introduce …	**En primer lugar, me gustaría presentarles …**
Would you like to say a few words about yourselves?	**¿Podrían decir algunas palabras sobre ustedes?**
Have you all got a copy of the agenda?	**¿Tienen todos una copia del orden del día?**
The objective/purpose/aim of this meeting is to …	**El objetivo/propósito/fin de esta reunión es …**
Now let's look at the agenda in detail.	**Ahora veamos más detalladamente el orden del día.**
As you can see there are four main points/items.	**Como pueden ver hay cuatro puntos/apartados principales.**
I think we will need about 30 minutes for point/item 1, 20 minutes for point/item 2, …	**Creo que necesitaremos unos 30 minutos para el primer punto/apartado, 20 minutos para el segundo punto/apartado, …**
We will break for coffee/for lunch at …	**Haremos un descanso para tomar un café/para comer a las …**
We aim to finish at … o'clock.	**Tenemos la intención de terminar a la(s) … en punto.**
Is that OK for everybody?	**¿Les parece bien a todos?**

Moving to points on the agenda

Let's look at the first point.	**Veamos el primer punto.**
I'd like to start with item one.	**Me gustaría empezar con el punto uno.**
OK, Rosa, over to you.	**Muy bien, Rosa, es tu turno.**
I believe you're going to lead this one.	**Creo que va usted a exponer este punto.**

NUMBERS, see page 17

Can I ask you to present the background information?	¿Puedo pedirle que presente la información general?
Right. Let's move on to the next point.	Bien. Pasemos al siguiente punto.
Felipe, would you like to introduce the next point?	Felipe, ¿te importaría presentar el siguiente punto?
OK, on to item 2.	Muy bien. Pasemos al punto 2.

Keeping the meeting on track

Inviting contributions

What's your opinion on this, Liz.	¿Cuál es tu opinión, Liz?
Juan, we haven't heard from you yet.	Juan, no has hablado todavía.
Would you like to add anything, José-Maria?	¿Quieres añadir algo, José-Maria?

Stopping people talking

We can't all speak at once. David first, then Liz, then Juan.	No podemos hablar todos a la vez. David primero, después Liz y luego Juan.
One at a time, please!	¡De uno en uno, por favor!
Well, thank you, José-Maria. I think that's clear now. Could we have some other opinions?	Bien, gracias José-Maria. Creo que ahora está todo claro. ¿Alguna otra opinión?

Dealing with problems of comprehension

I'm sorry. I didn't hear what you said. Would you mind repeating it, please?	Perdón. No he oído lo que ha dicho. ¿Le importaría repetirlo?
I'm sorry. I don't quite follow you.	Lo siento. No le he entendido muy bien.
Could you go over that again, please.	¿Puede repetirlo de nuevo, por favor?
What exactly do you mean by …?	¿Qué quiere decir con … exactamente?

SHOWING UNDERSTANDING, see page 47

Preventing irrelevance

I'm afraid that's outside the scope of this meeting.	**Me temo que eso no tiene que ver con los objetivos de esta reunión.**
We're beginning to lose sight of the main point.	**Estamos alejándonos del punto principal.**
Keep to the point, please.	**Cíñanse a la cuestión, por favor.**
We're running short of time.	**Se nos acaba el tiempo.**
Please be brief.	**Sea breve, por favor.**

Paraphrasing

So what you're saying is ...	**Lo que está diciendo es que ...**
In other words ...	**En otras palabras ...**
So you mean ...	**O sea, que ...**

Controlling decision-making

I'd like to (formally) propose that ...	**Me gustaría proponerles que ...**
Can we take a vote on that proposal?	**¿Podemos votar esa propuesta?**
All those in favour/favor. Right. All those against. Right, thank you.	**¿Quiénes están a favor? Bien. ¿Y en contra? Bien, gracias.**
So that motion has been accepted/rejected by 4 votes to 3.	**La moción ha sido aceptada/ rechazada por 4 votos a 3.**

Summarizing & minuting/recording

To sum up then, ...	**En resumen, ...**
So far we have agreed that ...	**Hasta ahora estamos de acuerdo en que ...**
Could you minute/record that, please?	**¿Puede tomar nota de esto, por favor?**
Have you minuted/recorded that?	**¿Ha apuntado eso?**

Concluding a point on the agenda

So, on point one we have agreed that ... we have accepted the figures.	**Bien. Sobre el punto uno estamos de acuerdo en que ...** **hemos aceptado las cifras.**

That leaves two follow-up tasks.	**Esto nos deja dos tareas a realizar.**
Paul, could you prepare some information for the next meeting?	**Paul, ¿puedes preparar información para la siguiente reunión?**
Felipe, when could we have the results of your survey?	**Felipe, ¿cuándo podemos tener los resultados del estudio?**
Well, I think that covers everything on that point.	**Bien. Creo que esto es todo sobre ese punto.**

Closing the meeting

Right. That just about covers everything.	**Bien. Con esto hemos terminado la reunión.**
So, the next meeting will be on … (date) at … (time).	**La siguiente reunión será el … a la(s) …**
I'll circulate the minutes of this meeting in the next few days.	**Les haré llegar las actas de esta reunión en los próximos días.**
Thanks for your participation.	**Gracias por su participación.**
Right, I declare the meeting closed.	**Se levanta la sesión.**

The Participants' role

Getting the chair's attention

(Mister/Madam) chairman.	**Señor/Señora presidente(-a).**
Excuse me for interrupting.	**Perdone que le interrumpa.**
May I come in here?	**¿Puedo hablar/intervenir?**
I'd like to comment on that.	**Me gustaría hacer un comentario.**

Giving opinions

strongly

I'm convinced/sure that …	**Estoy absolutamente convencido(-a)/seguro(-a) de que…**
I strongly believe that …	**Creo firmemente que …**
I definitely/certainly think that …	**No tengo ninguna duda de que …**

neutrally

I think/consider/feel that …	**Creo/Considero/Me parece que …**
As I see it, …	**Como yo lo veo, …**
From my point of view …	**Desde mi punto de vista …**

weakly

I'm inclined to think that …	**Me inclino a pensar que …**
I tend to think that …	**Tiendo a pensar que …**

Making recommendations

Shall we hear the figures now?	**¿Podemos ver las cifras ahora?**
Let's discuss the results first.	**Vamos a tratar primero los resultados.**
I suggest we postpone the decision till the next meeting.	**Sugiero que pospongamos la decisión hasta la próxima reunión.**

Agreeing or disagreeing with others

Full agreement

I totally agree with you.	**Estoy totalmente de acuerdo con usted.**
I'm in total agreement with you on that point.	**Coincido totalmente con usted en ese punto.**
I'm all in favour/favor of that proposal.	**Estoy totalmente a favor de esa propuesta.**

Partial agreement

Up to a point, I agree with you, but …	**Hasta cierto punto estoy de acuerdo con usted, pero …**
Of course, on the other hand …	**Desde luego, pero por otra parte …**
You could/may be right, but …	**Podría estar en lo cierto, pero …**

Disagreement

I don't agree with you on that point.	**No estoy de acuerdo con usted en ese punto.**
I can't accept that proposal.	**No puedo aceptar esa propuesta.**
I disagree totally.	**Estoy totalmente en desacuerdo.**

Conferences

congress	**el congreso**
symposium	**el simposio**
seminar	**el seminario**
convention	**la convención**
to attend	**asistir**
to participate	**participar**
chairperson	**el presidente(-a)**
participant	**el/la participante**
delegate	**el delegado(-a)**
speaker	**el orador(a), el/la ponente**
keynote speaker	**el orador(a) principal, el/la ponente principal**
presenter	**el presentador(a)**

Introducing the speaker

It gives me great pleasure to introduce Dr Jorge Gómez.	**Es un verdadero placer para mí presentarles al Dr. Jorge Gómez.**
I am very pleased to present Professor María Ríos.	**Me complace presentarles a la profesora María Ríos.**
He is going to present the findings of his latest research.	**Les hablará de los hallazgos de su última investigación.**
She will deliver a paper entitled 'Management 2000'.	**Va a distribuir entre ustedes un documento titulado 'Gestión 2000'.**

Research and findings

findings	**los hallazgos**
results	**los resultados**
conclusions	**las conclusiones**
outcome	**las consecuencias**

Addressing the audience

Ladies and gentlemen	**Señoras y señores**
It gives me great pleasure to address you today on ...	**Es un verdadero placer para mí dirigirme a ustedes hoy para ...**
I should also like to thank ... for sponsoring me.	**También me gustaría agradecer a ... por su patrocinio.**

INTRODUCTIONS, see page 23

COMMUNICATION SKILLS

Meetings, conferences and trade fairs

Thanking the speaker & inviting questions

I should like to thank Dr Jorge Gómez for his most interesting talk.	**Agradezco al Dr. Jorge Gómez su interesante exposición.**
Dr Gómez's talk touched many important issues.	**La exposición del Dr. Gómez ha tocado muchos temas importantes.**
So now, there will be an opportunity for questions.	**A continuación pueden hacer las preguntas que deseen.**
Are there any questions or comments.	**¿Alguna pregunta o comentario?**
Yes, your question, please.	**Sí, dígame.**

Concluding the talk

I'm afraid that I will have to interrupt this interesting discussion.	**Me temo que he de interrumpir este interesante debate.**
It is now time to move on to the next speaker.	**Ya es hora de pasar al siguiente ponente.**
We have scheduled a lunch break/coffee break until … o'clock.	**Hemos previsto un descanso para comer/tomar un café hasta la(s) … en punto.**
The next talk will start at … o'clock.	**La siguiente ponencia comenzará a la(s) … en punto.**

Concluding the conference

It has been a very interesting conference.	**Ha sido una conferencia muy interesante.**
We have heard a range of stimulating presentations.	**Hemos oído toda una serie de interesantes ponencias.**
It has been … inspiring intriguing provocative stimulating	**Ha sido muy …** **revelador** **fascinante** **provocador, sugestivo** **estimulante**
Finally, we look forward to seeing you all again next year in Miami.	**Finalmente, esperamos verles a todos de nuevo el año que viene en Miami.**

QUESTIONS AND ANSWERS, see page 36

Exhibitions and Trade Fairs

The Exhibitor's role

Introducing yourself and your company

Good morning/afternoon.	**Buenos días/Buenas tardes.**
My name's …	**Me llamo …**
Here's my card.	**Aquí está mi tarjeta.**
Do you know our company?	**¿Conoce nuestra empresa?**
I'm sure you know our organization.	**Estoy seguro(-a) de que conoce nuestra organización.**
We make/provide …	**Fabricamos/Suministramos …**
We are the largest company in our field.	**Somos la empresa más grande de nuestro sector.**

Finding out about your visitor

What do you do?	**¿A qué se dedica?**
Who do you work for?	**¿Para quién trabaja?**
What do they do?	**¿Qué es lo que hacen?**
Would you like some information about our products/services?	**¿Le gustaría tener más información sobre nuestros productos/servicios?**
Any specific product/service?	**¿Algún producto/servicio específico?**
What exactly would you like to know?	**¿Qué le gustaría saber exactamente?**

Giving information to the visitor

Please take a copy of our brochure/leaflet/prospectus.	**Coja [Lleve] un ejemplar de nuestro catálogo/folleto/prospecto.**
It contains all the product information.	**Contiene toda la información sobre el producto.**
We have a number of products which can …	**Tenemos varios productos que pueden …**
For your needs, I would recommend …	**Para sus necesidades, yo le recomendaría …**

GREETINGS, see page 23/INTRODUCING THE COMPANY, see page 28

This product/service …	Este producto/servicio …
is just right for your needs.	es lo más adecuado para satisfacer sus necesidades.
exactly covers your needs.	es exactamente lo que necesita.
could be the answer.	podría ser la respuesta.
may be able to solve your problem.	puede solucionar su problema.

I'm afraid we don't make anything like that.	Me temo que no hacemos nada parecido.
I'm sorry but we can't provide that service.	Lo siento, pero no podemos ofrecer ese servicio.

Planning follow-up action

Would you like …	¿Quiere que …
someone to visit your company?	alguien visite su empresa?
us to prepare a quotation?	le preparemos un presupuesto?
to discuss this over lunch/dinner/a coffee?	hablemos de ello en la comida/en la cena/tomando un café?
Would you like to return to the stand/booth later?	¿Le importa volver más tarde?
Would you like a demonstration of the equipment?	¿Le gustaría ver una demostración del equipo?
I/We'd be delighted to …	Me/Nos encantaría …
visit your company.	visitar su empresa.
prepare a quotation.	preparar un presupuesto.
discuss this later.	hablar de ello más adelante.

Saying good-bye

We'll be in touch with you next week/month.	Nos pondremos en contacto con usted la semana/el mes que viene.
Good-bye.	Adiós.

The Visitor's role

Explaining your areas of interest

I am interested in …	Estoy interesado(-a) en …

INTRODUCING THE PRODUCT, see page 31

| I would like to know more about ... | Me gustaría tener más información sobre ... |

Questioning the exhibitor

Could you explain exactly ...	¿Le importaría explicarme exactamente ...
what this product does?	qué hace este producto?
how this machine works?	cómo funciona esta máquina?
where this service is provided?	dónde puedo obtener este servicio?
if this service is available here?	si puedo obtener aquí este servicio?

Planning follow-up action

I/We would like ...	Me/Nos gustaría ...
someone to visit our company.	que alguien visite nuestra empresa.
to have a quotation.	tener un presupuesto.
to discuss this further.	hablar de ello más adelante.
to see a demonstration.	ver una demostración.

| I look forward to hearing from you. | Espero verle pronto. |

Communication difficulties

| Could you speak ... | ¿Puede hablar ... |
| a bit slower/louder, please? | un poco más despacio/alto, por favor? |

| I'm sorry, could you repeat that, please. | Perdón, ¿podría repetírmelo, por favor? |

| What exactly do you mean by ...? | ¿Qué quiere decir exactamente con ...? |

| Could you explain that, please? | ¿Podría explicármelo, por favor? |

Showing understanding

I see.	Ya entiendo.
I understand.	Comprendo.
Yes, I've got that now.	Sí, ahora lo entiendo.
Yes, that's clear now.	Sí, ahora está claro.

NEGOTIATIONS

Check-list

To help you prepare your negotiation, it is useful to plan it around the following stages:

1. Creating the right environment	☐	**1. Creación del ambiente adecuado**
2. Defining the issues	☐	**2. Definición de los temas**
3. Establishing opening positions	☐	**3. Establecimiento de las posiciones iniciales**
4. Handling the offer and counter-offer	☐	**4. Manejo de ofertas y contraofertas**
5. Testing the other side's case	☐	**5. Estudio de la posición de la otra parte.**
6. Strengthening your case	☐	**6. Refuerzo de sus argumentos**
7. Handling stalemate	☐	**7. Manejo de puntos muertos**
8. Clinching the deal	☐	**8. Conclusión del asunto**
9. Getting it in writing	☐	**9. Ponerlo por escrito**
10. The legal aspects	☐	**10. Los aspectos legales.**

The processes

to negotiate	**negociar**
to bargain	**tratar**
to discuss	**hablar de**
to persuade	**persuadir**
to compromise	**comprometer(se)**
to make a deal	**hacer un trato**
to strike a bargain	**cerrar el trato**
to reach agreement	**llegar a un acuerdo**
to draft a contract	**hacer un borrador de un contrato**
to sign the contract	**firmar el contrato**
to implement the agreement	**llevar a la práctica el acuerdo**
to break the contract	**romper el contrato**

The subject of negotiation

price	**el precio**
delivery and terms	**la entrega y los plazos**

payment and credit	el pago y el crédito
discount	el descuento
licences/licenses	las licencias
warranties and guarantees	las garantías y los avales
penalties	las sanciones
legal jurisdiction	la jurisdicción legal

1. Creating the right environment

For key phrases for introducing yourself and making small talk, see Section 1 Making Contact: Introductions and Socializing.

2. Defining the issues

Stating the agenda

OK. Shall we start?	Muy bien. ¿Podemos empezar?
Our position is as follows:	Nuestra posición es la siguiente:
We would like to buy ...	Nos gustaría comprar ...
We are interested in selling ...	Estamos interesados en vender ...
We need to reach agreement about ...	Necesitamos llegar a un acuerdo sobre ...
We are eager to make a decision about ...	Tenemos que tomar una decisión respecto a ...
The aim/purpose/objective of this negotiation is to solve the problem over ...	El fin/propósito/objetivo de esta negociación es resolver el problema de ...

Clarifying the agenda

So, if we understand you correctly, you want to sell ...	Entonces, si no entendemos mal, quieren vender ...
So, are we right in thinking that you would like us to sell ...?	Entonces, si estamos en lo cierto, les gustaría que vendamos ...
We fully understand your views/position ...	Entendemos totalmente su postura/punto de vista ...
but what would you actually like us to do?	pero, ¿qué es lo que quiere que hagamos en realidad?
but what precisely are you offering?	pero, ¿qué es lo que nos están ofreciendo realmente?

INTRODUCTIONS, see page 23/SOCIALIZING, see page 25

3. Establishing opening positions

Price

In your proposal, ...	En su propuesta, ...
your asking price is ...	su precio de oferta es ...
you have set the price at ...	el precio establecido es ...
We are willing to pay ...	Estamos dispuestos a pagar ...
Our initial offer is ...	Nuestra oferta inicial es ...

Delivery and terms

In addition, ...	Además, ...
we/you can deliver the goods on July 25th.	podemos/pueden entregar la mercancía el 25 de julio.
we can supply the products by July 25th.	podemos suministrar los productos hacia el 25 de julio a més tardar.
Our position is that we need the goods by July 20th.	Nuestra posición es que necesitamos la mercancía hacia el 20 de julio como tarde.
Can you arrange delivery to our site by truck?	¿Podrían organizar la entrega en nuestras instalaciones por camión?
However, you expect us to provide transport and insurance.	Sin embargo, esperan que cubramos el transporte y el seguro.
However, you do not agree to pay for ...	Sin embargo, no aceptan pagar ...

Payment and credit

We expect payment by bank transfer ...	Esperamos el pago mediante transferencia bancaria ...
within 60 days.	en un plazo de 60 días.
90 days after invoice.	a 90 días de la fecha de la factura.
90 days after order.	90 días después de la fecha del pedido.
Our normal payment terms are by letter of credit.	Nuestras condiciones de pago normales son mediante carta de crédito.

PAYMENT, see page 76/DISTRIBUTION, see page 71

COMMUNICATION SKILLS

Negotiations

Do you accept our payment terms?	**¿Aceptan nuestras condiciones de pago?**

We do not normally pay ...
  in cash
  by bank transfer
	Normalmente no pagamos ...
	  en efectivo, en metálico
	  mediante transferencia bancaria

Discount

However, we can offer an initial discount of 5%.	**Sin embargo, podemos ofrecer un descuento inicial del 5%.**
But we are prepared to reduce the total price by 5%.	**Pero estamos dispuestos para reducir el precio total en un 5%.**
What discount can you offer?	**¿Qué descuento pueden ofrecernos?**

Licences/Licenses

What licence/license can you offer?	**¿Qué licencia pueden ofrecer?**
We are prepared to offer a licence/license to sell the product.	**Estamos dispuestos a ofrecer una licencia para la venta del producto.**
We cannot grant a licence/license to manufacture the product.	**No podemos conceder licencias para la fabricación del producto.**
The licence/license will initially be limited to 5 years.	**Inicialmente, la licencia será limitada a 5 años.**

Warranties and guarantees

What warranties and guarantees do you offer?	**¿Qué garantías y avales ofrecen?**
We warrant the goods for a period of 5 years.	**Garantizamos la mercancía durante un período de 5 años.**
We cover all parts and labour/labor for 1 year.	**Cubrimos las piezas y la mano de obra durante 1 año.**

In that case, we ...
  will replace the goods.
  will repair the equipment free of charge.
	En ese caso, ...
	  sustituiremos la mercancía.
	  repararemos el equipo sin cargo alguno [gratuitamente].

PRICING, see page 84/DATES, see page 15

We cannot guarantee the goods against ...	No podemos garantizar la mercancía contra ...
breakdown	averías
normal wear and tear	uso y desgaste normales

Penalties

What happens if anything goes wrong?	¿Qué ocurre si algo va mal?
What compensation will you pay if ...?	¿Qué indemnización pagarán si ...?
We will claim compensation if ...	Reclamaremos indemnización si ...
you don't deliver on time	no hacen la entrega a tiempo
the goods are delayed	la mercancía se retrasa
the equipment breaks down	el equipo se avería

Legal jurisdiction

What happens if there is a dispute?	¿Qué ocurre en caso de controversia?
Any disputes will be settled according to Spanish [Mexican] law.	Cualquier pleito se resolverá de conformidad con la legislación española [mexicana].
We resolve any disagreements by arbitration.	Resolveremos cualquier desacuerdo mediante arbitraje.

4. Handling the offer and counter-offer

Positive

That's great.	Está bien.
(That's a) good/excellent/great idea.	(Esa es una) idea buena/excelente/brillante.
We accept/agree.	Aceptamos./Estamos de acuerdo.
We can accept your payment/delivery/discount terms.	Podemos aceptar las condiciones del pago/de la entrega/del descuento.
We are in agreement over penalty clauses.	Estamos de acuerdo con las cláusulas de penalización.

Partial

Yes, but ...	Sí, pero ...

LEGAL DEPARTMENT, see page 78/CONTRACT LAW, see page 121

We're on the right track.	**Estamos en el buen camino.**
We're getting there.	**Estamos en vías de encontrar una solución.**

Negative

That's unacceptable.	**Eso es inaceptable.**
That's out of the question.	**Eso es imposible.**
We can't accept that.	**No podemos aceptarlo.**
We don't agree to that.	**No estamos de acuerdo con esto.**
We are not in agreement over compensation clauses.	**No estamos de acuerdo en las cláusulas de indemnización.**

5. Testing the other side's case

Have you given us all the relevant facts?	**¿Nos ha proporcionado todos los hechos relacionados?**
On what are those figures based?	**¿En qué se basan estas cifras?**
We have heard that ...	**Hemos oído que ...**
your normal prices are ...	**sus precios normales son ...**
normal delivery terms are ...	**sus condiciones normales de entrega son ...**
Could you explain how you reach ...?	**¿Podría explicar cómo ha llegado a ...?**
We don't follow the logic of your argument.	**No seguimos la lógica de su argumento.**
If your normal prices are ..., then we expect ...	**Si sus precios normales son ..., esperamos ...**
Could you explain how you got to those figures?	**¿Podría explicar como ha llegado a esas cifras?**

6. Strengthening your case

If we accept ...	**Si aceptamos ...**
your prices, then we will have to raise our prices.	**sus precios, tendremos que elevar los nuestros.**
your payment terms, that will increase our costs.	**sus condiciones de pago, tendremos que aumentar nuestros costes [costos].**
That will not be good for our business.	**Eso no sería un buen negocio para nosotros.**

GIVING OPINIONS, see page 41

If you can reduce your price by ..., then we will ...	**Si pudieran reducir su precio en ..., nosotros podríamos ...**
If you are prepared to speed up delivery by ..., then we will ...	**Si estuvieran preparados para agilizar la entrega en ..., nosotros podríamos ...**
If you are willing to reconsider your payment terms, then we will ...	**Si estuvieran dispuestos a reconsiderar sus condiciones de pago, nosotros podríamos ...**
look at prices for our next contract.	**revisar los precios para nuestro próximo contrato.**
review delivery for the next consignment.	**revisar la entrega del siguiente envío.**

7. Handling stalemate

We are very far apart on this issue.	**Nuestras posiciones están muy alejadas sobre este particular.**
Our positions are very different on the question of ...	**Nuestras posturas son muy diferentes respecto a ...**
I don't think we can resolve this matter now.	**No creo que podamos resolver este asunto ahora.**
Let's see where we agree ...	**Veamos en qué estamos de acuerdo ...**
Shall we summarise the points of agreement ...	**Hagamos un resumen de los puntos de acuerdo ...**
and then take a short break.	**y hagamos un breve descanso.**
and then adjourn till this afternoon.	**y suspendamos la reunión hasta esta tarde.**
So far, we've agreed on the following points: ...	**Hasta ahora, estamos de acuerdo en los siguientes puntos: ...**
We disagree on ...	**Estamos en desacuerdo en ...**
So we'll come back to those issues after the break.	**Volveremos a estos temas después del descanso.**

8. Clinching the deal

We have covered a lot of ground in this meeting.	**Hemos resuelto muchos temas en esta reunión.**
We cannot change our offer.	**No podemos cambiar nuestra oferta.**

This is our final offer.	Ésta es nuestra oferta final.
We have/have not reached agreement on ...	Hemos/No hemos llegado a un acuerdo sobre ...
You have accepted our terms on ...	Ustedes han aceptado nuestras condiciones de ...
You cannot accept our terms on ...	Ustedes no pueden aceptar nuestras condiciones de ...
Let me go over all the details again.	Permítanme repasar todos los detalles otra vez.
Have I covered everything?	¿Me he olvidado de algo?
Do you agree?	¿Están de acuerdo?
Do you accept these terms?	¿Aceptan estas condiciones?

9. Getting it in writing

I will draft an outline agreement.	Haré un borrador de contrato.
Can you prepare a draft contract?	¿Pueden preparar un borrador de contrato?
I will send the agreement to you for your comments.	Les enviaré el contrato para que lo lean y formulen sus omentarios.
Please send the draft contract to me for our comments.	Envíenme el borrador de contrato para poder hacer comentarios.
After the contract/agreement has been signed, we can ...	Una vez firmado el contrato/ acuerdo, podemos ...
make the goods.	fabricar los productos.
deliver the equipment.	entregar el equipo.

10. The legal aspects

contract	el contrato
parties to the contract	las partes del contrato
to sign a contract	firmar un contrato
signatories to the contract	los signatarios del contrato
scope of the contract	el ámbito del contrato
terms of the contract	las condiciones del contrato
clauses of the contract	las cláusulas del contrato
breach of contract	el incumplimiento de contrato
indemnity	la indemnización
force majeure	la fuerza mayor

CONTRACT LAW, see page 121/LEGAL JURISDICTION, see page 52

PROJECTS AND PERFORMANCE

> **Check-list**
>
> To help you manage your project better, it is useful to plan it around the following stages or milestones:
>
> 1. Defining objectives ❏ **1. Definición de objetivos**
>
> 2. Prioritizing and sequencing ❏ **2. Prioridad y orden de**
>   activities **las actividades**
>
> 3. Allocating resources ❏ **3. Asignación de recursos**
>
> 4. Evaluating performance ❏ **4. Evaluación del rendimiento**
>
> 5. Project completion ❏ **5. Finalización del proyecto**

Project types

Company reorganization	**la reorganización de la empresa**
Company restructuring	**la reestructuración de la empresa**
Automation project	**el proyecto de automatización**
IT project	**el proyecto de tecnología informática [de la información]**
Cost control project	**el proyecto de control de costes [costos]**
Quality project	**el proyecto de control de calidad**
Research project	**el proyecto de investigación**
Installation project	**el proyecto de instalación**
Construction project	**el proyecto de construcción**
Product launch	**el lanzamiento de productos**

The project team

The team consists of a ...	**El equipo consta de un ...**
We have appointed a ...	**Hemos nombrado a un ...**
project leader	**director(a) de proyecto**
project supervisor	**supervisor(a) de proyecto**
project manager	**jefe(-a) de proyecto**
project assistant	**ayudante(-a) de proyecto**
project secretary	**secretario(-a) de proyecto**

1. Defining objectives

What exactly do we want to achieve?	¿Qué es lo que queremos lograr exactamente?
How exactly are we going to achieve it?	¿Cómo vamos a lograrlo exactamente?
Is this project really necessary?	¿Es este proyecto realmente necesario?
The aims/objectives/goals of this project are to ...	Los objetivos/propósitos/fines de este proyecto son ...
In this project, we ...	En este proyecto, ...
aim to ...	pretendemos ...
plan to ...	pensamos ...
mean to ...	queremos ...
propose to ...	proponemos ...
intend to ...	tenemos la intención de ...
reorganize the company	reorganizar la empresa
increase output	aumentar la producción
introduce new equipment	introducir nuevos equipos
launch an updated product	lanzar un producto actualizado

2. Prioritizing and sequencing activities

The stages

The project consists of 10 phases.	El proyecto consta de 10 fases.
The project will be divided into 10 stages/activities.	El proyecto se dividirá en 10 etapas/actividades.
At the end of each stage, there is a milestone.	Al final de cada etapa, hay una fecha de entrega.
The phases and milestones are shown on this project schedule.	Las fases y las fechas de entrega aparecen en este calendario del proyecto.
You can see the phases ...	Pueden ver las fases ...
on the critical path analysis	en el análisis del camino crítico
on the flowchart	en el diagrama de flujo
on the Gantt chart	en el diagrama de Gantt

Questions about the schedule

When are we due to start the project?	¿Cuándo debemos empezar el proyecto?

VISUAL AIDS, see page 35

When will the first stage be finished?	¿Cuándo hay que terminar la primera fase?
How long will the first activity take?	¿Cuánto tiempo durará la primera actividad?
When do we plan to complete the whole project?	¿Cuándo se piensa terminar el proyecto?

Details about the schedule

The first stage will start on July 25th.	La primera etapa comenzará el 25 de julio.
We will begin this activity on July 25th.	Empezaremos esta actividad el 25 de julio.
This phase will take 3 weeks.	Esta fase tardará 3 semanas.
This stage will last until August 4th.	Esta etapa durará hasta el 4 de agosto.
The next stage will be to ...	La siguiente etapa será ...
The whole project must be completed by April 15th.	El proyecto completo debe terminar hacia el 15 de abril.

Prioritising

The most important activity is ...	La actividad más importante es ...
The most critical activity is ...	La actividad más crítica es ...
The key stages are ...	Las etapas clave son ...
The major stages are ...	Las etapas principales son ...

Project activities

collecting the data	la recogida de datos
interpreting the data	la interpretación de los datos
researching the market	el estudio de mercado
designing the prototype	el diseño del prototipo
testing the prototype	la comprobación del prototipo
selecting the subcontractors	la selección de subcontratistas
recruiting the workforce	la contratación de personal
subcontracting the manufacture of components	la subcontratación de la fabricación de componentes
producing the equipment	la producción del equipo
choosing an advertising agency	la selección de una agencia de publicidad
agreeing the promotion	el acuerdo de la promoción

DATES, see page 15

finalizing the launch date	**el establecimiento de la fecha de lanzamiento**
building the foundations	**la cimentación**
installing the equipment	**la instalación del equipo**
starting up the plant	**la puesta en marcha de la fábrica**
handing over the plant	**la entrega de la fábrica**

3. Allocating resources

Forecasting

I am sure/convinced that ...	**Estoy seguro(-a)/convencido(-a) de que ...**
we will need more time.	**necesitaremos más tiempo.**
It is likely that ...	**Es probable que ...**
we will need more money.	**necesitemos más dinero.**
We may ...	**Puede que ...**
need more people.	**necesitemos más personas.**
We are unlikely to ...	**No es probable que ...**
need more equipment.	**necesitemos más equipos.**
We definitely/certainly won't ...	**Definitivamente no ...**
need more materials.	**necesitamos más materiales.**

Time

How much time will we need?	**¿Cuánto tiempo necesitaremos?**
How long do we have for the first stage?	**¿Cuánto tiempo tenemos para la primera etapa?**
We will need ...	**Necesitamos ...**
more/less time than budgeted.	**más/menos tiempo del previsto.**
a longer time for stage 1.	**más tiempo para la etapa 1.**
a shorter time for stage 2.	**menos tiempo para la etapa 2.**
another 3 days for stage 3.	**otros 3 días para la etapa 3.**
We need to complete this phase in spring/summer/autumn (fall)/winter.	**Tenemos que terminar esta fase en primavera/verano/otoño/invierno.**

Budget

How much will it cost?	**¿Cuánto costará?**
What is the budget?	**¿Cuál es el presupuesto?**
We will need more money than allocated.	**Necesitaremos más dinero que el asignado.**

TIME, see also page 15/FINANCE DEPARTMENT, see page 73

It will cost more than budgeted.	**Costará más de lo previsto.**
We forecast it will cost another 500,000 pesetas [pesos].	**Prevemos que costará otras [otros] 500.000 pesetas [pesos].**

People

How many people do we need?	**¿Cuántas personas necesitamos?**
We don't have enough people.	**No tenemos suficientes personas.**
Should we use our people or can we subcontract some of the work out?	**¿Debemos arreglarnos con nuestra gente o podemos subcontratar parte del trabajo?**
We will need to employ/hire some extra …	**Tenemos que emplear/contratar algunos …**
operators	**operadores**
specialists	**especialistas**
technicians	**técnicos**
workers	**trabajadores**
We plan to subcontract some of the work out.	**Pensamos subcontratar fuera parte del trabajo.**

Responsibilities

The project leader has overall responsibility for …	**El director(a) del proyecto tiene la responsabilidad general de …**
The project supervisor is in charge of …	**El supervisor(a) del proyecto está encargado(-a) de …**
The project manager will take care of …	**El jefe(-a) del proyecto estará al cuidado de …**
The project assistant is responsible for …	**El ayudante(-a) del proyecto es responsable de …**
The project secretary will support/assist the project leader.	**El secretario(-a) del proyecto apoyará/ayudará al director del proyecto.**
financial questions	**las cuestiones financieras**
personnel matters	**los asuntos de personal**
day-to-day administration	**la administración diaria**
accommodation on site	**el alojamiento en las instalaciones**
contracts with suppliers	**los contratos con los proveedores**
dealing with contractors	**tratar con los contratistas**

COMPANY POSITIONS, see page 28

| buying in materials | comprar materiales |
| organizing transport | organizar el transporte |

Materials

What materials do we need?	¿Qué materiales necesitamos?
Do we have the necessary equipment?	¿Disponemos del equipo necesario?
We don't have enough materials/equipment.	No tenemos equipo suficiente/ materiales suficientes.
We can produce the materials in-house.	Podemos producir los materiales nosotros mismos.
We need to buy in the materials.	Tenemos que comprar los materiales.
What equipment do we need to hire/lease/buy?	¿Qué equipos necesitamos alquilar/arrendar/comprar?

4. Evaluating performance

The project

How is the project going?	¿Cómo marcha el proyecto?
The project is on target.	El proyecto marcha según lo previsto.
We are ahead of schedule.	Estamos más avanzados de lo previsto.
We are behind schedule.	Estamos retrasados con respecto a lo previsto.
The costs are as forecast.	Los costes [costos] son los previstos.
The costs are running above/ below budget.	Los costes [costos] están por encima/debajo del presupuesto.
We have had a cost overrun.	Nos hemos excedido en los costes [costos].
We are facing some difficulties/ problems with ...	Se nos han presentado algunas dificultades/algunos problemas con ...
the timing of the project.	los plazos del proyecto.
the financing of the project.	la financiación del proyecto.
the manpower for the project.	la mano de obra para el proyecto.
the equipment for the project.	el equipo para el proyecto.

| We can't … | No podemos … |
| recruit the right workers. | contratar los trabajadores adecuados. |

| We need to review the situation. | Tenemos que revisar la situación. |

We need to look again at …	Tenemos que replantearnos …
the schedule.	el calendario.
the budgets.	los presupuestos.
our manpower needs.	nuestras necesidades de mano de obra.
our material requirements.	nuestros requisitos de material.

| We must control costs. | Debemos controlar los costes [costos]. |

We need to …	Tenemos que …
lay off some of the workers.	despedir algunos trabajadores.
fire the supervisor.	despedir al supervisor(a).

Personal qualities

The project leader is …	El director(a) del proyecto es muy …
efficient	eficiente
effective	eficaz
hard-working	trabajador(a)
competent	competente
conscientious	concienzudo(-a)
ambitious	ambicioso(-a)

The project supervisor is …	El supervisor(a) del proyecto es …
logical	lógico(-a)
methodical	metódico(-a)
analytical	analítico(-a)
rational	racional(a)
calm	tranquilo(-a)
inflexible	inflexible
good with facts and figures	hábil(a) con cifras y números

The project manager is …	El jefe(-a) del proyecto es …
practical	práctico(-a)
energetic	enérgico(-a)
dynamic	dinámico(-a)
single-minded	resuelto(-a)
impatient	impaciente
good at negotiating	hábil(a) para las negociaciones

The project designer is …	El diseñador(a) del proyecto es …
creative	creativo(-a)
imaginative	imaginativo(-a)
unorthodox	poco(-a) ortodoxo(-a)
impractical	poco(-a) práctico(-a)
The project assistant is …	El ayudante(-a) del proyecto es …
sympathetic	simpático(-a)
perceptive	perceptivo(-a)
communicative	comunicativo(-a)
good at developing team relationships	hábil(a) para las relaciones entre el equipo

Business trends

to increase/to raise
to put up/to step up
   We have increased the budget for stage one.

**aumentar/elevar
incrementar/subir**
   Hemos aumentado el presupuesto para la etapa uno.

an increase/a rise
   We have to budget for an increase in the cost of materials.

un aumento/una subida
   Tenemos que presupuestar un aumento en el coste [costo] de los materiales.

to decrease/to cut
to reduce
   We have cut the budget for phase two.

**disminuir/recortar
reducir**
   Hemos recortado el presupuesto para la fase dos.

dramatic(ally)	espectacular(mente)
vast(ly)	inmenso (-amente)
huge(ly)	terrible(mente)
enormous(ly)	enorme(mente)
substantial(ly)	sustancial(mente)
considerable (considerably)	considerable(mente)
significant(ly)	significativo (-amente)
moderate(ly)	moderado (-amente)
slight(ly)	ligero (-amente)
a little	un poco

to fall/to drop	**caer/disminuir**
to go down/to slump	**estar por debajo/descender**
The manpower costs have fallen.	***Los costes [costos] de mano de obra han descendido.***
a fall/a drop	**una caída/una disminución**
a cut/a reduction	**un recorte/una reducción**
a collapse/a slump	**un colapso/un descenso**
We estimate there will be a decrease in the cost of materials.	***Estimamos que habrá una disminución en el coste [costo] de los materiales.***
to hold ... stable	**mantener estable ...**
to maintain ... at the same level	**mantener ... al mismo nivel**
We have kept costs constant during the project.	***Hemos mantenido constantes los costes [costos] durante el proyecto.***
to remain constant	**permanecer constante**
to stay stable	**permanecer estable**

5. Project completion

We have finished the project.	**Hemos finalizado el proyecto.**
The plant is operational.	**La fábrica es operativa.**
The product is ready for launch.	**El producto está listo para su lanzamiento.**
We are ready to ...
start up the new equipment.	**Estamos preparados para ...
poner en marcha el nuevo equipo.**
We have managed to ...
increase output.	**Hemos ...
aumentado la producción.**
Congratulations. We have completed the project successfully.	**Felicidades. Hemos terminado el proyecto satisfactoriamente.**
Well done. You have achieved your objective/target.	**Enhorabuena. Han conseguido cumplir sus objetivos/fines.**
I'd like to thank the project team for their ...
hard work during the project
commitment (to ...)
collaboration (in ...)
participation (in ...)	**Me gustaría agradecer al equipo su ...
esfuerzo durante el proyecto
compromiso (con ...)
colaboración (en ...)
participación (en ...)**

Company Departments

ADMINISTRATION

Administrative staff

administrator	**el administrador(a)**
clerk	**el administrativo(-a)**
office manager	**el jefe(-a) de oficina**
personal assistant	**el secretario(-a) personal**
she's the personal assistant to the Managing Director/CEO	***es la secretaria personal del director ejecutivo***
secretary	**el secretario(-a)**
typist	**el mecanógrafo(-a)**

Information organization

archive (n)	**el archivo**
we keep the old records in the archives	***mantenemos los registros antiguos en los archivos***
file (n)/(v)	**el archivo/archivar**
have you filed that letter?	***¿ha archivado esa carta?***
filing cabinet	**el archivador**
photocopier	**la fotocopiadora**
sort (v)	**clasificar**

CUSTOMER SERVICE

agent	el/la representante
he acts as agent for us in Australia	*es nuestro representante en Australia*
busy	ocupado(-a)
cater for/serve	suministrar, abastecer, proveer, servir
we cater for/serve a wide range of customers	*servimos a un gran número de clientes*
custom	la clientela
customer	el cliente(-a)
customize	hacer a la medida
all our products are customized	*todos nuestros productos se hacen a la medida*
deal (n)/(v)	la transacción/tratar
delay (n)	el retraso, la demora
we're sorry for the delay	*lamentamos la demora*
demand (n)	la demanda
we can't keep up with demand	*no podemos satisfacer la demanda*
discontinue	cancelar
I'm afraid this line has been discontinued	*me temo que esta línea se ha cancelado*
exchange (n)/(v)	el intercambio/intercambiar
exempt (adj)	exento(-a)
these products are VAT/sales tax exempt	*estos productos están exentos del IVA*
export (n)/(v)	la exportación/exportar
fetch/pick up	llevar, servir
we'll fetch/pick up the order this afternoon	*serviremos el pedido esta tarde*
file (n)	el archivo
we keep all our customers on file	*mantenemos un archivo de todos nuestros clientes*
customer file	el archivo de clientes
handle (v)	manejar
import (n)/(v)	la importación/importar
install	instalar
when would you like the equipment installed?	*¿cuándo quiere tener instalado el equipo?*

DISTRIBUTION, see page 71

item	el artículo
the order consists of four items	*el pedido consta de cuatro artículos*
label	la etiqueta
off-peak hours	horas *f* de valle
off-season	fuera de temporada, temporada baja
paperwork	el papeleo
there's a lot of paperwork to do	*hay mucho de papeleo por hacer*
part-exchange	el intercambio de piezas
quality	la calidad
quantity	la cantidad
run out of	agotarse
I'm afraid we've run out of those items	*me temo que estos artículos se han agotado*
scarce	escaso(-a)
schedule (n)/(v)	el plan/planificar
we've scheduled delivery for the end of the month	*hemos planificado la entrega para finales del mes*
service	el servicio
the service is slow	*el servicio es lento*
after-sales service	el servicio postventa
service industry	el sector de servicios
tariff	la tarifa
triplicate	triplicado(-a)
the order form needs filling out in triplicate	*hay que rellenar el formulario de pedido por triplicado*

Negotiating

bargain (n)/(v)	la ganga/regatear
barter (n)/(v)	el trueque/hacer negocios de trueque
conditions of sale	las condiciones de venta
our conditions of sale are printed on the back of the invoice	*nuestras condiciones de venta están impresas en la cara posterior de la factura*
haggle	regatear
negotiate	negociar

NEGOTIATIONS, see page 48

negotiable	**negociable**
these terms are not negotiable	***estas condiciones no son negociables***
negotiation	**la negociación**

Complaints

blame (n)/(v)	**el reproche/culpar**
claim (n)/(v)	**la reclamación/reclamar**
the customer has made a claim for damages	***el cliente ha reclamado daños***
compensate	**compensar, indemnizar**
damage	**el daño**
the accident caused a lot of damage	***el accidente provocó un gran daño***
damages	**los daños**
fault/defect (n)	**el fallo**
guarantee (n)	**la garantía**
the guarantee lasts a year	***la garantía dura un año***
hazard	**el peligro**
insure	**asegurar**
insurance claim	**la reclamación del seguro**
insurance cover	**la cobertura del seguro**
insurance policy	**la póliza de seguro**
does your policy cover this claim?	***¿su póliza cubre esta reclamación?***
insurance premium	**la prima del seguro**
overdue	**vencido(-a), pendiente, retrasado(-a)**
the delivery is overdue	***la entrega se ha retrasado***
repair (n)	**la reparación**
spoil	**deteriorar**
the goods were spoiled in transit	***la mercancía se deterioró durante el transporte***

Payment

credit	**el crédito, el abono**
credit note	**la nota de crédito/de abono**
hire purchase	**la compra a plazos**

PAYMENT, see also page 76

invoice (n)/(v)	la factura/facturar
you'll be invoiced at the end of the month	*se le facturará a final de mes*
lease (n)/(v)	el alquiler/alquilar
outright purchase	la compra en firme
over-charged	el recargo, el cargo excesivo
overpaid	el pago excesivo
you've overpaid so we'll send you a credit note	*ha pagado un cargo excesivo, por lo que le enviaremos una nota de abono*
pay (v)	pagar
pay by cheque/check	pagar mediante cheque
pay in cash	pagar en efectivo/en metálico
payable	pagadero/(-a)
this invoice is payable in 30 days	*la factura es pagadera a 30 días*
payment	el pago
we demand payment in advance	*exigimos el pago por adelantado*
prepaid	prefranqueado(-a)
please enclose a prepaid envelope	*tenga la bondad de incluir un sobre prefranqueado*
rebate	el descuento, la rebaja
settle	saldar, pagar
could you settle the bill in advance?	*¿podría pagar la cuenta por adelantado?*
statement	el estado de cuenta
we will send you a monthly statement	*le enviaremos un estado de cuenta mensual*

Orders

acknowledge	acusar recibo, confirmar
the order was acknowledged on June 30	*la fecha de acuse de recibo del pedido es el 30 de junio*
acknowledgment	el acuse de recibo, la confirmación
availability	la disponibilidad
bring forward/move up	adelantar
we'd like to bring forward/ move up the delivery date	*nos gustaría que adelantaran la fecha de entrega*

bulk	al por mayor
we offer 10% discount for bulk orders	*ofrecemos un 10% de descuento en pedidos al por mayor*
cancel	cancelar
cancellation	la cancelación
confirm	confirmar
could you please confirm your order in writing?	*¿podrían confirmar su pedido por escrito, por favor?*
notify	notificar, avisar
we'll notify you of any delay	*les notificaremos cualquier retraso*
offer (n)/(v)	la oferta/ofrecer
order (n)	el pedido
fulfil an order	despachar un pedido
on order	bajo pedido
we've got 25 on order	*se han pedido 25*
back order	el pedido pendiente
place an order	hacer un pedido
are you ready to place an order?	*¿están preparados para hacer un pedido?*
postpone	posponer
I'm afraid we'll have to postpone our order	*me temo que tendremos que posponer nuestro pedido*
quote (v)	presupuestar
could you quote us for 500 units?	*¿podría presupuestarnos 500 unidades?*
quotation	el presupuesto
how long is your quotation valid for?	*¿hasta cuándo es válido el presupuesto?*
ready	preparado(-a)
receive	recibir
receipt	el recibo
could you let me have a receipt?	*¿podría extenderme un recibo?*
reorder	repetir el pedido
a repeat order	un nuevo pedido
shortage	el déficit, la insuficiencia
there's a severe shortage of stock	*tenemos un grave déficit de existencias*
in stock/out of stock	en existencias/sin existencias

DISTRIBUTION

by boat/ferry/ship/tanker	por barco/transbordador/buque/petrolero
by post/special delivery/airmail	por correo/correo urgente/correo aéreo
by truck/van/train	por camión/furgoneta/ferrocarril
cargo	la carga
carriage/freight	el transporte
the price includes carriage	*el precio incluye el transporte*
cif (cost, insurance and freight)	c.i.f. (coste [costo], seguro y flete)
crate	el cajón de embalaje
deliver	entregar
delivery	la entrega
delivery note	la nota de entrega
there should be a delivery note with the invoice	*deberá haber una nota de entrega junto con la factura*
delivery time	la fecha de entrega
28 days delivery time	*entrega en 28 días*
depot	el almacén, la estación
dispatch (v)	despachar
distribute	distribuir
duty	el impuesto, el arancel
enclose	adjuntar
please find enclosed our price list	*adjunto le enviamos nuestra lista de precios*
envelope	el sobre
f.o.b. (free on board)	f.a.b. (franco a bordo)
forward (v)	expedir
could you forward the goods to the distributor?	*¿podrían expedir la mercancía al distribuidor?*
freight	el flete
in transit	durante el transporte
the order was lost in transit	*el pedido se perdió durante el transporte*
lading, bill of	el conocimiento de embarque
load (v)	cargar
the goods were loaded onto the trucks	*la mercancía se cargó en los camiones*
mail (n)/(v)	el envío/enviar por correo
pack (v)	embalar

package (n)	el embalaje
pallet	el palet, la plataforma
ship (v)	enviar
have you shipped the goods?	*¿han enviado la mercancía?*
shipment	el envío
unload	descargar

Channels

branch	la sucursal
there is a branch in every major town	*hay una sucursal en todas las ciudades importantes*
chain	la cadena
this store is part of a chain	*esta tienda es parte de una cadena*
channel	el canal
our main distribution channel is via the wholesaler to the retailer	*nuestro canal de distribución principal es del mayorista al minorista*
consignment	el envío
we're expecting a consignment later today	*esperamos un envío a última hora de hoy*
dealer	el distribuidor, el concesionario(-a)
department store	los grandes almacenes [las grandes tiendas]
direct export	la exportación directa
franchise (n)	la franquicia
middleman	el intermediario(-a)
network	la red
we're building a dealer network	*estamos creando una red de distribuidores*
quota	la cuota
retail (adj)	al por detalle, al menor
retail outlet	el punto de venta al por menor
retailer	el minorista
scarce	escaso(-a)
storage	el almacenamiento
tariff	la tarifa
warehouse	el almacén
wholesale (n)	la venta al por mayor

FINANCE

accounts	las cuentas
the monthly accounts show all the figures	*las cuentas mensuales muestran todas las cifras*
accountancy	la contabilidad
accountant	el/la contable [el contador(a)]
acquire	adquirir
acquisition	la adquisición
advance (n)/(v)	el adelanto/adelantar
backing	el apoyo, el respaldo
they need some financial backing	*necesitan cierto apoyo financiero*
backdate	antefechar
the cheque/check was backdated	*el cheque estaba antefechado*
black, in the	con ganancia, en números negros
books, keep the	llevar los libros
borrow	pedir un préstamo
break even (v)	equilibrar
break-even point	el punto de equilibrio
we've reached the break-even point	*hemos llegado al punto de equilibrio*
budget (n)/(v)	el presupuesto/presupuestar
we've budgeted for a loss	*hemos presupuestado una pérdida*
capital	el capital
cash	el efectivo, el metálico, la caja
cheque/check	el cheque
cost	el coste [costo]
fixed/variable/running	fijo/variable/corriente
credit (n)	el crédito
currency	la moneda
debt	la deuda
debtor	el deudor
deduct	deducir
defer	aplazar
the taxation can be deferred until next year	*la tributación puede aplazarse hasta el año próximo*
due	debido(-a)
earn	ganar

BANKING, see page 115

earnings	las ganancias
annual earnings exceeded our forecast	*las ganancias anuales superaron nuestras previsiones*
finance (n)/(v)	las finanzas/financiar
they are willing to finance the project	*están dispuestos a financiar el proyecto*
funds	los fondos
income	los ingresos
interest	el interés
interest rate	el tipo de interés
interest rates were cut by ½%	*los tipos de interés se recortaron en un 0,5%*
lend	prestar
lender	el/la prestamista
loan (n)	el préstamo
overdraw	girar en descubierto
overdraft	el sobregiro, el giro en descubierto
our overdraft facility is 2 million pesetas [pesos]	*nuestro servicio de sobregiro es de 2 millones de pesetas [pesos]*
owe	adeudar
petty cash	la caja para gastos menores, la caja chica
profit (n)	el beneficio
profitable	rentable
profitability	la rentabilidad
rate	la tasa
recover	recuperar
red, in the	con déficit, en números rojos
rough estimate	la estimación aproximativa
save (v)	ahorrar
savings	los ahorros
subsidize	subvencionar
subsidy	la subvención, el subsidio

Investment

base rate	el tipo base
terms are 2% above base rate	*las condiciones son 2 puntos por encima del tipo base*
bond	el bono

broker	el corredor(a) de bolsa
our broker advised us to sell our shares	*nuestro corredor nos aconsejó que vendiéramos nuestras acciones*
dealer	el operador(a) de balsa
dividend	el dividendo
they announced the same dividend as last year	*presentaron los mismos dividendos que el año anterior*
earnings per share	los beneficios por acción
equity	el capital propio
gross yield	el rendimiento bruto
invest	invertir
investment	la inversión
portfolio	la cartera
you should have some oil shares in your portfolio	*su cartera debería contener algunas acciones petroleras*
portfolio management	la gestión de carteras
premium (n)	la prima
securities	los valores
the securities market can be very volatile	*el mercado de valores puede ser muy volátil*
share/stock	la acción
shareholder/stockholder	el/la accionista

Financial statements

asset	el activo
current assets	el activo circulante
fixed assets	el inmovilizado, el activo fijo
intangible assets	el inmovilizado inmaterial, el activo fijo intangible
audit (n)	la auditoría
auditor	el auditor
balance sheet	el balance
the balance sheet looks sound	*el balance parece saludable*
cash flow	el flujo de caja
negative cash flow	el flujo de caja negativo
debit (n)	el debe, el débito
depreciate	depreciar, amortizar
these assets are depreciated over 3 years	*estos activos se han depreciado en tres años*

FINANCIAL PROBLEMS, see page 80

Finance

depreciation	la depreciación, la amortización
expenditure	el gasto
expenses	los gastos
goodwill	el fondo de comercio
goodwill is included under intangible assets	*el fondo de comercio se incluye bajo el inmovilizado inmaterial*
gross (adj)	bruto(-a)
gross margin	el margen bruto
gross profit	el beneficio bruto
half-yearly results	los resultados semestrales
inventory	las existencias, el inventario
ledger	el libro mayor
sales/purchase ledger	el libro mayor de ventas/compras
liabilities	el pasivo
current liabilities	el pasivo circulante
margin	el margen
overheads	los gastos generales
our overheads are too high	*nuestros gastos generales son demasiado elevados*
profit and loss account/ income statement	la cuenta de pérdidas y ganancias
quarterly	trimestralmente
reserves	las reservas
results	los resultados
retained earnings	los beneficios no distribuidos
return (n)	la rentabilidad
return on investment	la rentabilidad de la inversión
turnover/sales	el volumen de negocios, la facturación
annual turnover/sales has doubled over 5 years	*nuestro volumen de negocios anual se ha doblado en 5 años*
working capital	el capital circulante
write-off (n)/(v)	la cancelación/cancelar
this asset has now been written off	*este activo ha sido cancelado*

Payment

| bad debt | la deuda incobrable |
| *this invoice has been posted as a bad debt* | *esta factura se ha contabilizado como deuda incobrable* |

PAYMENT, see also page 68

bank charges	los gastos bancarios
bank draft/check	el giro bancario
bank statement	el extracto bancario
blank cheque/check	el cheque en blanco
bounce (v)	ser sin fondos
the cheque/check bounced	*era un cheque sin fondos*
convert (v)	convertir
credit limit	el límite de crédito
credit rating	la clasificación crediticia
direct debit	el débito directo
demand (n)	la demanda
discount (n)	el descuento
invoice (n)/(v)	la factura/facturar
letter of credit	la carta de crédito
we will pay by letter of credit	*pagaremos mediante carta de crédito*
outstanding	pendiente
500,000 pesetas [pesos] is still outstanding	*tenemos un saldo pendiente de 500.000 pesetas [pesos]*

Tax

capital gains tax	el impuesto sobre plusvalías
corporation tax	el impuesto de sociedades
declare	declarar
tax declaration	la declaración fiscal
income tax	el impuesto sobre la renta [el impuesto a los ingresos, el impuesto a los réditos]
taxable	imponible
is this purchase taxable?	*¿esta compra es imponible?*
tax allowance	la desgravación fiscal
tax deductible	deducible a efectos fiscales, desgravable
tax evasion	la evasión fiscal
tax loophole	la laguna impositiva
tax relief	la desgravación fiscal
you can get tax relief	*puede obtener una desgravación fiscal*
value added tax *(sales tax)*	el impuesto sobre el valor añadido [agregado] (IVA)

LEGAL

abide by	respetar
abuse (n)/(v)	el abuso/abusar
abuse of power	el abuso de poder
appeal (n)/(v)	la apelación/apelar
arbitrate	arbitrar
arbitration	el arbitraje
the dispute has gone to arbitration	la disputa se ha sometido a arbitraje
bequest (n)	el legado
the property was left to her as a bequest	la propiedad pasó a ella como un legado
bond	la fianza
civil law	el derecho civil
claim (n)/(v)	la demanda/demandar
they have a claim	tienen una demanda
claimant	el/la demandante
conflict of interest	el conflicto de intereses
copyright	el copyright [los derechos de propiedad intelectual]
court	el tribunal [la corte]
go to court	ir a juicio
we're going to court	iremos a juicio
damages	los daños
fee	los honorarios
illegal/legal	ilegal/legal
indemnify	indemnizar
indemnity	la indemnización
infringe copyright	infringir las leyes del copyright [de la propiedad intelectual]
infringement	la infracción
irrevocable letter of credit	la carta de crédito irrevocable
judicial	judicial
jurisdiction	la jurisdicción
this contract comes under British jurisdiction	este contrato se somete a la jurisdicción británica
law	la ley
within/outside the law	dentro/fuera de la ley
against the law	contra la ley
legal department	el departamento legal/jurídico

CONTRACT LAW, see page 121/EMPLOYMENT LAW, see page 122

liability	la responsabilidad
limited liability	la responsabilidad limitada
litigant	el/la litigante, el/la querellante
loophole, tax	la laguna impositiva
party	la parte
third party	el tercero
patent (n)	la patente
file a patent application	presentar una solicitud de patente
penalty	la multa, la penalización
penalty clause	la cláusula de penalización
the contract included a penalty clause for late completion	*el contrato incluye una cláusula de penalización por demora*
pledge (n)/(v)	la promesa/prometer
precedent	el precedente
there is no precedent for this decision	*no hay ningún precedente de esta decisión*
settlement	el arreglo, el acuerdo
out of court settlement	el acuerdo extrajudicial
settle out of court	arreglar extrajudicialmente
sue	demandar
we can sue them for non-payment	*podemos demandarles por falta de pago*
suit	el pleito
trademark	la marca registrada
tribunal	el tribunal
unlawful	ilegal
waive	renunciar
the company decided to waive its usual fee in this case	*la empresa decidió renunciar a sus honorarios habituales en este caso*

People

actuary	el actuario
advocate	el abogado(-a)
attorney/barrister	el procurador(-a), el abogado(-a)
bailiff/sheriff	el alguacil
lawyer	el abogado(-a)
legal advisor	el asesor(a) legal
solicitor	el abogado(-a)

Crimes

break the law	violar la ley
bribe	sobornar
bribery	el soborno
embezzle	malversar
he embezzled all the company's profits	*malversó todos los beneficios de la empresa*
embezzlement	la malversación
extort	extorsionar
extortion	la extorsión
fraud	el fraude
he was accused of fraud	*fue acusado de fraude*
fraudulent	fraudulento(-a)
kickback	la comisión ilegal
misconduct	la mala conducta
professional misconduct	la mala conducta profesional
swindle (n)	la estafa

Financial problems

bankrupt (adj)	en quiebra
to go bankrupt	quebrar
bankruptcy	la quiebra, la bancarrota
debt	la deuda
foreclose	entablar juicio hipotecario, ejecutar la hipoteca
the bank foreclosed on the property	*el banco entabló un juicio hipotecario sobre la propiedad*
foreclosure	el juicio hipotecario, la ejecución de la hipoteca
insolvent	insolvente
insolvency	la insolvencia
liquidate	liquidar
liquidation	la liquidación
the company has gone into liquidation	*la compañía ha entrado en liquidación*
liquidator	el administrador(a) judicial
receiver	el síndico(-a)
a receiver has been appointed to sell off the assets	*se ha nombrado un síndico para vender los activos*
receivership	la liquidación

MARKETING

capture market share	**la captura de la cuota de mercado**
cartel	**el cártel**
client	**el cliente(-a)**
compete	**competir**
competition	**la competencia**
competitor	**el competidor(-a)**
competitive	**competitivo(-a)**
competitive pricing	**el precio competitivo**
domestic market	**el mercado interno**
down-market	**de calidad inferior**
end-user	**el usuario(-a) final**
we sell direct to the end-user	**vendemos directamente al usuario final**
exhibit (v)	**exponer**
exhibition	**la exposición**
flop (n)	**el fracaso**
the launch was a complete flop	**el lanzamiento fue un completo fracaso**
forecast (v)	**pronosticar**
we forecast that we will become market leaders next year	**pronosticamos que el año que viene nos convertiremos en líderes del mercado**
goodwill	**el fondo de comercio**
logo	**el logotipo, el emblema**
market (n)	**el mercado**
market leader	**el líder de mercado**
market niche	**el hueco/área del mercado**
they have found a profitable market niche	**han encontrado un área de mercado muy rentable**
market penetration	**la penetración en el mercado**
market segmentation	**la segmentación del mercado**
market share	**la cuota de mercado**
mass-market	**el mercado masivo**
outlet	**el punto de venta**
we have a retail outlet in most major cities	**tenemos un punto de venta al por menor en la mayoría de las ciudades importantes**
resistance	**la resistencia**
there is some price resistance	**hay cierta resistencia de precios**

SALES DEPARTMENT, see page 96

saturate	saturar
sector	el sector
segment	el segmento
share (n)	la cuota (de mercado)
survey (n)	el estudio
target (n)/(v)	el objetivo/destinar
up-market	de primera calidad
it's an upmarket product	*se trata de un producto de*
aimed at the luxury sector	*primera calidad dirigido al sector*
	de artículos de lujo

Products

benefit (n)	el beneficio
brand (n)	la marca
brand leader	la marca líder
brand loyalty	la fidelidad a una marca
brand loyalty will stop	*la fidelidad a la marca evitará*
customers switching to	*que los clientes cambien a*
generic products	*productos genéricos*
by-product	el subproducto
diversify	diversificar
feature (n)	la característica
flagship product	el producto estrella
generic	genérico(-a)
giveaway	el regalo publicitario
goods	la mercancía, los artículos
industrial	industrial
label	la marca
private label products are	*los artículos de marca se están*
selling well	*vendiendo bien*
launch	el lanzamiento
life cycle	la duración
positioning	el posicionamiento
product line/range	la línea/la gama de productos
prototype	el prototipo
seasonal	estacional
sell-by date	la fecha de caducidad
this product has passed its	*este producto ha caducado*
sell-by date	
shelf-life	la duración útil en almacén
tailor-made	hecho(-a) a medida

trade mark	**la marca registrada**
white goods	**los electrodomésticos**

Advertising

account executive	**el ejecutivo(-a) de cuentas**
advertise	**promocionar**
advertisement	**la promoción**
art director	**el director(a) de arte**
artwork	**las ilustraciones**
audience	**el público**
the ad has to reach a certain audience	***el anuncio [el aviso] tiene que llegar a determinado público***
banner	**el rótulo**
body copy	**el texto del anuncio [del aviso]**
brief (n)	**los órdenes, las instrucciones**
broadsheet	**el gran formato**
we're going to advertise in the broadsheet and tabloid press	***vamos a anunciarnos [publicar avisos] en periódicos de gran formato y tabloides***
brochure	**el folleto**
campaign	**la campaña publicitaria**
canvass	**dirigirse a**
we have canvassed a lot of potential customers	***nos hemos dirigido a gran cantidad de clientes potenciales***
caption	**la frase publicitaria**
catalogue/catalog	**el catálogo**
this product is not included in our current catalogue/catalog	***este producto no está incluido en nuestro catálogo actual***
circular	**la circular**
endorse	**respaldar**
endorsement	**el respaldo**
endorsement by a well-known actress will boost sales	***el respaldo de una actriz conocida disparará las ventas***
flier	**el folleto**
freesheet	**la hoja suelta**
issue (n)	**el número, la edición**
jingle	**la melodía**
the ad has a very catchy jingle	***el anuncio [el aviso] tiene una melodía muy pegadiza***
layout	**el diseño, la maquetación**

magazine	la revista
we'll reach our audience through magazines	*conseguiremos llegar a nuestro público mediante revistas*
media	los medios de comunicación
mass media	los medios de comunicación de masas
media coverage	la cobertura informativa
outdoor advertising	la publicidad en exteriores
we've designed some posters for outdoor advertising	*hemos diseñado algunos carteles para publicidad en exteriores*
pamphlet	el panfleto
periodical	el periódico
poster	el cartel (publicitario)
prospectus	el prospecto
the company issued a shareholder prospectus	*la compañía ha publicado un prospecto para accionistas*
publication	la publicación
ratings	los índices
weekly TV ratings	los índices semanales de TV
readership	los lectores
slogan	el eslogan [el slogan]
slot	la cuña publicitaria
spot	el spot [el aviso] publicitario
TV spot	el spot [el aviso] de TV
spread (n)	el anuncio [el aviso] a doble página
sticker (n)	la pegatina [la calcomanía]
viewer	el telespectador(a)
voice-over	la voz en off

Pricing

bargain (n)	la ganga
ceiling	el máximo autorizado, el tope
price ceiling	el precio máximo
cut-price rate/cut-rate price	el precio reducido
cut-price deals have reduced margins	*las operaciones con precios reducido han disminuido los márgenes*
discount (n)	el descuento

elastic	elástico(-a)
fix (v)	fijar
going rate	la tarifa actual
we should charge the going rate	*cargaremos la tarifa actual*
gross margin	el beneficio bruto
index, retail price	el índice del precios al por menor
inelastic	inflexible
introductory offer	la oferta introductoria
knockdown/mask-down (adj)	de saldo
margin	el margen
mark up (v)/(n)	subir/la subida
the retailer has marked up the price by 50%	*el minorista ha subido el precio un 50%*
MRP (Manufacturer's Recommended Price)	el precio recomendado por el fabricante
overheads	los gastos generales
premium (n)	la prima
rate (n)	el tipo
refund (n)/(v)	reintegrar/el reintegro
retail price	el precio al por menor
surcharge (n)	el sobreprecio
value (n)	el valor

Public relations

identity	la identidad
corporate identity	la identidad corporativa
image	la imagen
corporate image	la imagen corporativa
lobby (v)	presionar
we are lobbying the Minister for/Secretary of Agriculture	*estamos presionando al Ministro de Agricultura*
press officer	el encargado(-a) de relaciones con la prensa
press relations	las relaciones con la prensa
press release	el comunicado de prensa
we have issued a press release	*hemos publicado una nota de prensa*
sponsor (v)	patrocinar
sponsorship	el patrocinio

PERSONNEL

absent	ausente
absenteeism	el absentismo
absenteeism has risen due to bad health	*el absentismo se ha elevado debido a la mala salud*
canteen	el restaurante de empresa
career	la carrera
conditions	las condiciones
working conditions	las condiciones de trabajo
conditions of employment	las condiciones de empleo
core time	el horario obligatorio
core time is between 10:00 and 15:00	*el horario obligatorio es entre las 10:00 y las 15:00*
employ	emplear
employee	el empleado(-a)
employer	el empresario(-a)
equal opportunity	la igualdad de oportunidades
this company has an equal opportunities policy	*en esta empresa tienen una política de igualdad de oportunidades*
flexitime	el horario flexible
hire	contratar
human resources	los recursos humanos
job centre/center	el centro de trabajo
job sharing	compartir puesto de trabajo y sueldo
job satisfaction	la satisfacción laboral
leader	el líder
leadership	el liderazgo
we are looking for leadership qualities	*estamos buscando a una persona con cualidades de líder*
manpower	la mano de obra
manpower planning	la planificación de la mano de obra
pool (n)	el grupo
secretaries are drawn from a pool	*se utilizan las secretarias de un grupo*
position (n)	el cargo
punctuality	la puntualidad
shift (n)	el turno
night shift	el turno de noche

shopfloor	el taller
sick note	el parte de baja [la licencia] por enfermedad
trade union	el sindicato
vacation	las vacaciones
working hours	las horas laborales
working hours are currently 37 per week	*la semana laboral es actualmente de 37 horas*
work load	la carga de trabajo

Types of jobs

blue-collar worker	el trabajador(a) manual
board of directors	el consejo de administración [el directorio]
clerk	el administrativo(-a) [el/la oficinista]
management	la dirección
middle management	la gerencia intermedia
manager	el directivo
manual (adj)	manual
manual worker	el trabajador(a) manual
skilled	cualificado(-a)
semi-skilled/unskilled	semicualificado(-a)/no cualificado(-a)
shift workers	los trabajadores de turnos
staff	la plantilla
subordinate (n)	el subordinado(-a)
superior (n)	el superior
his superior reports to the Managing Director/CEO	*su superior depende del director gerente*
white-collar worker	el trabajador(a) de oficina/ de cuello blanco

Disputes

grievance	el motivo de queja
their grievances include low pay and long hours	*sus motivos de queja son el bajo salario y la cantidad de horas de trabajo*
industrial action	la acción laboral
industrial relations	las relaciones laborales

COMPANY POSITIONS, see page 28/EMPLOYMENT LAW, see page 122

Personnel

industrial unrest	el desorden laboral
picket (n)/(v)	el piquete/organizar piquetes
the factory was picketed during the strike	*durante la huelga, se organizaron piquetes en la fábrica*
strike (n)	la huelga
be on strike	estar en huelga
go on strike	ponerse en huelga, declarar la huelga
work-to-rule	la huelga de celo

Recruitment

applicant	el/la aspirante, el/la solicitante
application form	el formulario de solicitud
apply for a job	solicitar un trabajo
appoint	nombrar
candidate	el candidato(-a)
curriculum vitae/resumé	el curriculum vitae
experience (n)	la experiencia
fill (a position)	cubrir (un puesto)
induction/training	la formación en prácticas
interview, to come for	ir a una entrevista
interviewee	el entrevistado(-a)
interviewer	el entrevistador(a)
job description	la descripción del trabajo
qualifications	las titulaciones
qualified	cualificado(-a)
we're only interested in qualified personnel	*sólo estamos interesados en personal cualificado*
well-qualified/unqualified	bien cualificado(-a)/ no cualificado(-a)
recruit (v)	contratar
recruitment	la contratación
reference	la referencia
they followed up her references	*comprobaron sus referencias con más detalle*
select	seleccionar
shortlist (v)	preseleccionar
vacancy	la vacante
I'm afraid we have no vacancies at present	*me temo que no necesitamos mano de obra por el momento*

Leaving

dismissal	**el despido**
fire (v)	**despedir**
he was fired for stealing	***se le despidió por robo***
hand in one's notice	**presentar la dimisión**
lay-off (n)/(v)	**el despido/despedir**
2,000 workers will be made redundant/laid off	***se reducirá la plantilla en 2.000 trabajadores***
resign	**dimitir**
resignation	**la dimisión**
retire	**retirarse, jubilarse**
retirement	**la jubilación, el retiro**
he was offered early retirement	***se le ofreció la jubilación anticipada***

Assessment

appraise/review	**evaluar**
all the staff are appraised/ reviewed annually	***anualmente se evalúa a toda la plantilla***
appraisal/review	**la evaluación**
competence	**la competencia**
grade (n)	**el grado**
perform	**rendir**
performance appraisal	**la evaluación de rendimiento**
probation	**el período de prueba**
he's on probation for 6 months	***está en un período de prueba de 6 meses***

Training & development

apprentice	**el aprendiz(a)**
the company takes on 5 apprentices a year	***la empresa contrata a 5 aprendices al año***
apprenticeship	**el aprendizaje**
course	**el curso**
facilitate	**facilitar**
the training should facilitate decision-making	***la formación debería facilitar la toma de decisiones***
mentor	**el tutor(a)**
on-the-job training	**la formación en prácticas**

promote	promocionar
progress (v)	progresar
seminar	el seminario
we are organizing a seminar on leadership skills	*estamos organizando un seminario sobre técnicas de liderazgo*
train (v)	formar
training	la formación
workshop	el taller

Remuneration

benefit (n)	el beneficio
fringe benefit	el pago en especie
company cars are a common fringe benefit	*los coches de empresa son un pago en especie habitual*
sickness benefit	el subsidio por enfermedad
collective bargaining	el convenio colectivo
compensate	compensar
deduction	la deducción
my take-home pay after all deductions is very little	*mi sueldo neto después todas las deducciones es muy bajo*
incentive	el incentivo
income	los ingresos
overtime	las horas extraordinarias [extra]
you can make up the wage with overtime	*puede aumentar su salario con horas extraordinarias [extra]*
pay (n)/(v)	el sueldo/pagar
pay package	el paquete salarial
payroll	la nómina
pension	la pensión
perk	el beneficio adicional
profit-sharing	la participación en beneficios
the employees all benefit from a profit-sharing scheme	*todos los empleados tienen una participación en beneficios*
raise (n)/(v)	el aumento/aumentar
I just received a salary raise	*acabamos de recibir un aumento salarial*
reward (n)	el premio
salary	el salario
wage	el salano, el jornal

PRODUCTION

Quality

accurate	preciso(-a)
accuracy	la precisión
assess	valorar
defect	el defecto
the defect was caused by a faulty machine	el defecto se debió a una máquina averiada
evaluate	evaluar
inspect	inspeccionar
ISO	ISO
quality (assurance/control) circle	el grupo de control de calidad
the plant has set up quality circles	la planta ha establecido grupos de control de calidad
reject (n)/(v)	el producto defectuoso/rechazar
the reject rate has fallen as a result of quality control	el porcentaje de productos defectuosos ha disminuido como resultado del control de calidad
scrap (n)/(v)	los residuos/tirar
zero defect	cero defectos
we are aiming for zero defect production	pretendemos conseguir una producción con cero defectos

Process

assemble	montar
assembly	el montaje
assembly line	la línea de montaje
the assembly line has been automated	la línea de montaje se ha automatizado
automate	automatizar
automation	la automatización
component	el componente, la parte
continuous process	el proceso continuo
convert	convertir
efficiency	la eficiencia
efficient	eficiente
finished goods	los artículos elaborados/ terminados

goods	**los artículos**
intermittent production	**la producción intermitente**
line assembly	**el montaje en línea**
line worker	**el trabajador de una línea**
off-the-shelf	**disponible en almacén**
produce (v)	**producir**
production	**la producción**

Planning

backlog	**los pedidos pendientes**
there is a backlog of orders to deal with	*tenemos una gran cantidad de pedidos pendientes*
batch (n)	**el lote**
capacity	**la capacidad**
we are working at full capacity	*estamos trabajando a plena capacidad*
critical path analysis	**el análisis del camino crítico**
cycle time	**el tiempo de un ciclo**
delivery cycle	**el período de entrega**
downtime	**el tiempo de parada**
machine downtime costs money	*el tiempo de parada de las máquinas cuesta dinero*
flow rate	**la medida del gasto**
idle	**parado(-a)**
we can't afford for the machines to be idle	*no podemos permitirnos que las máquinas estén paradas*
job lot	**el lote suelto de mercancías**
lead time	**el tiempo de espera para la entraga**
the lead time is too long	*el tiempo de espera para la entraga es demasiado largo*
make-to-order	**la fabricación según pedido**
make to stock	**fabricar según existencias**
output (n)	**la producción**
productive	**productivo(-a)**
productivity	**la productividad**
productivity levels have increased	*los niveles de productividad han aumentado*
prototype	**el prototipo**
schedule (n)	**el plan**

set-up time	el tiempo de preparación de una máquina
slack (n)	el tiempo de demora previsible
throughput	la capacidad de producción, el rendimiento
work-in progress	el trabajo en curso

Resources & stock

bill of materials	la lista de materiales
equip	equipar
equipment	el equipamiento
inventory	el inventario
just-in-time	justo a tiempo
machine	la máquina
machinery	la maquinaria
MRP (Materials Requirements Planning)	la planificación de materiales necesarios
materials handling	la manipulación de materiales
raw materials	las materias primas
stock (n)	las existencias, el stock
stock levels	los niveles de stock
in stock/out of stock	en stock/agotado(-a)
we have just one left in stock	*sólo nos queda una en stock*
stock control	el control de existencias
store (n)/(v)	las existencias acumuladas/ acumular
storage	el almacenamiento

Maintenance

break down	averiarse
this machine has never broken down	*esta máquina nunca se ha averiado*
failure	la avería
fault	el fallo
faulty	defectuoso(-a)
maintain	mantener
maintenance	el mantenimiento
repair (v)	reparar
reliable	fiable [confiable]
reliability	la fiabilidad [la confiabilidad]
shut-down/shut down	la parada/pararse

PURCHASING

auction (n)	la subasta
buy	comprar
buyer	el/la agente de compras
junior/senior	ayudante/superior
purchaser	el comprador(a)
source	el proveedor(a)
you should have at least two sources	*deberá tener dos proveedores como mínimo*
spend (n)/(v)	el gasto/gastar
total purchasing spend is over 1 million	*el gasto total en compras es de más de 1 millón*
supply (v)	suministrar
supplies	los suministros
we buy in supplies	*compramos suministros*
supplier	el proveedor(a)
vendor	el vendedor(a)

Functions

inventory management	la gestión de inventario
inventory control	el control de inventario
logistics	la logística
materials management	la gestión de materiales
vendor appraisal	la evaluación del vendedor
the criteria for vendor appraisal include price, quality and delivery	*los criterios de evaluación de un vendedor incluyen el precio, la calidad y los plazos de entrega*

Finance

bill (n)	la factura
billing	la facturación
we prefer quarterly billing	*preferimos la facturación trimestral*
currency	la moneda
weak/strong currency	la divisa débil/fuerte
currency fluctuations	las fluctuaciones monetarias

Supply & demand

buyers'/sellers' market	el mercado favorable al comprador/vendedor

demand (n)	la demanda
under-demand	la baja demanda
prices are low because of under-demand	*los precios son bajos a causa de la baja demanda*
over-demand	el exceso de demanda
supply (n)	la oferta
under-supply	la oferta insuficiente
over-supply	el exceso de oferta

Tendering process

accept	aceptar
our offer was accepted	*nuestra oferta ha sido aceptada*
call (n) for tenders	la convocatoria de ofertas
the call for tenders was published in the press	*la convocatoria de ofertas se publicó en la prensa*
open/closed tender	la oferta abierta/cerrada
reject (v)	rechazar
submit a tender/an offer	enviar una oferta
tender specifications	las especificaciones de la oferta
the tender specifications are very detailed	*las especificaciones de la oferta son muy detalladas*
tender evaluation	la evaluación de ofertas

Documents

letter of intent	la carta de intenciones
we sent the supplier a letter of intent	*enviamos al proveedor una carta de intenciones*
purchase order	la orden de compra

Price negotiation

bottom-line	el precio mínimo
our bottom-line was £150,000	*nuestro precio mínimo era de 150.000 libras esterlinas*
cut (n)	el recorte
we forced a 10% price cut on all our suppliers	*hemos conseguido un recorte de precios del 10% de todos nuestros proveedores*
margin	el margen
target price	el precio indicativo

SALES

client/customer	el cliente(-a)
end-user	el usuario(-a) final
give-away	el regalo publicitario
we usually supply give-aways such as pens	*normalmente distribuimos regalos publicitarios como plumas*
prospect	el posible cliente(-a)
he's a good prospect	*es un posible cliente muy importante*
sales call	la visita comercial
I've got one more sales call to make	*tengo que hacer otra visita comercial*
sales conference	la conferencia de ventas
target	el objetivo
we have a very ambitious sales target this year	*este año tenemos un objetivo de ventas muy ambicioso*
sample (n)	la muestra

Selling people & organisation

field sales	el/la representante de ventas
we've got a team of 3 field salespeople	*tenemos un equipo de 3 representantes de ventas*
sales area	el área de ventas
the country is divided into four sales areas	*el país está dividido en cuatro áreas de ventas*
sales assistant/manager	el ayudante(-a)/director(-a) de ventas
salesforce	el equipo de vendedores

Types of selling

door-to-door sales	la venta a domicilio
direct sales	la venta directa
hard selling	la venta agresiva
hard selling doesn't work in this business	*la venta agresiva no funciona en este tipo de negocio*
personal selling	la venta personal
soft selling	la venta por persuasión
telephone sales	la venta por teléfono

Industries and Professions

CONSTRUCTION

Materials used in construction

asphalt	**el asfalto**
brick	**el ladrillo**
red brick	**el ladrillo rojo**
cement	**el cemento**
clay	**la arcilla**
concrete	**el hormigón**
pre-fabricated concrete	**el hormigón prefabricado**
reinforced concrete	**el hormigón armado**
glass	**el cristal**
frosted glass	**el cristal esmerilado**
plain glass	**el vidrio fundido sin burbujas**

reinforced glass	el cristal reforzado
safety glass	el cristal de seguridad
gravel	la grava
macadam	el macadam
masonry	la mampostería
mortar	la argamasa
plastic	el plástico
slate	la pizarra
steel	el acero
steel girder	las vigas de acero
stone	la piedra
cobble stone	el guijarro, el canto rodado
tarmac	la superficie asfaltada
tiles	las tejas
timber	el maderamen
uPVC	el uPVC
wood	la madera
wooden beam	la viga de madera
wooden plank	la plancha de madera

Planning regulations in this area prohibit the use of prefabricated concrete.

La normativa de planificación en esta zona prohibe el uso de hormigón prefabricado.

Professions in construction

architect	el arquitecto(-a)
brick layer	el albañil
builder	el constructor(a)
carpenter	el carpintero(-a)
designer	el diseñador(a)
developer	el promotor de viviendas
draughtsman	el/la dibujante
engineer	el ingeniero(-a)
civil	de caminos
sanitary	sanitario(-a)
structural	de estructuras
glazier	el cristalero(-a)
joiner	el ebanista
painter	el pintor(a)
planner	el proyectista
plasterer	el yesista, el revocador(a)
plumber	el fontanero(-a)
	[el plomero(-a)]

PROPERTY, see page 110

| surveyor | el agrimensor(a) |
| quantity surveyor | el aparejador(a) [el inspector(a) de materiales] |

Our on-site management team consists of an architect, responsible for drawing up the plan, a civil engineer and a surveyor.

Nuestro equipo de obra consta de un arquitecto, responsable de dibujar los planos, un ingeniero de caminos y un aparejador [un inspector de materiales].

Processes in construction

to build	edificar, construir
to chart	cartografiar
to construct	construir
to cool	refrigerar
to demolish	demoler
to design	diseñar
to dig	cavar
to draft	bosquejar
to draw	dibujar
to erect	levantar
to excavate	excavar
to heat	instalar de la calefacción
to install	instalar
to maintain	mantener
to measure	medir
to plan	trazar planos
to refurbish	reformar
to renovate	renovar
to repair	reparar
to replace	sustituir
to scaffold	construir andamios
to sketch	hacer croquis
to ventilate	ventilar
to wire	instalar cables

Our company specializes in refurbishing old houses: everything from designing the plans to carrying out the job.

Nuestra empresa está especializada en reformar casas antiguas: desde el diseño de planos hasta la realización de las obras.

ENGINEERING

Branches of engineering

architectural engineering	**la ingeniería arquitectónica**
chemical engineering	**la ingeniería química**
civil engineering	**la ingeniería de caminos**
drainage engineering	**la ingeniería de tratamiento de aguas**
electrical engineering	**la ingeniería eléctrica**
electronic engineering	**la ingeniería electrónica**
fire protection engineering	**la ingeniería de protección contra incendios**
highway engineering	**la ingeniería de caminos**
hydraulic engineering	**la ingeniería hidráulica**
industrial engineering	**la ingeniería industrial**
marine engineering	**la ingeniería naval**
mechanical engineering	**la ingeniería mecánica**
mining and metallurgical engineering	**la ingeniería de minas y metalúrgica**
nuclear engineering	**la ingeniería nuclear**
petroleum production engineering	**la ingeniería petrolera**
production engineering	**la ingeniería de producción**
railway engineering	**la ingeniería ferroviaria**
safety engineering	**la ingeniería de seguridad (talleres)**
sanitary engineering	**la ingeniería sanitaria**
structural engineering	**la ingeniería de estructuras**
welding engineering	**la ingeniería de soldaduras**

We plan to call in a safety engineering company to advise us on improving standards.

Pensamos hacer intervenir una empresa de ingeniería de dispositivos de seguridad para que nos aconsejen sobre la mejora de las normas.

Applications of engineering

boiler	**la caldera**
boring	**el sondeo**
bridge	**el puente**
dye (n)	**el colorante**
electricity supply	**el suministro eléctrico**
gas manufacture	**la explotación de gas**

hydraulics	la hidráulica
mining	las minas
paper manufacture	la fabricación de papel
power generation	la generación de energía
power transmission	la transmisión de energía
printing	la imprenta
shipbuilding	la construcción de barcos/ buques

Equipment in engineering

boiler	la caldera
crane	la grúa
gas engine	el motor de gas
machine tools	las máquinas herramienta
pump	la bomba
turbine/engine	la turbina
steam	de vapor
water	de agua

This boiler has an auxiliary safety valve to prevent a build-up of pressure.

Esta caldera tiene una válvula de seguridad auxiliar para evitar el exceso de presión.

Processes in treating metals

to anneal	recocer
to anodize	anodizar
to electroplate	electrochapar
to forge	forjar
to found	fundir
to galvanize	galvanizar
to grind	rectificar con muela abrasiva
to harden	endurecer, templar
to mint	acuñar
to plate	electrodepositar
to roll	laminar
to temper	templar
to terneplate	alear
to tinplate	estañar

Some of our customers ask us to galvanize the metal in order to strengthen it.

Algunos de nuestros clientes nos piden que galvanicemos el metal con objeto de reforzarlo.

FOOD AND CATERING

The meals

breakfast	el desayuno
lunch	la comida
dinner	la cena
picnic	la merienda campestre [el picnic]
snack	el aperitivo

The elements of food

carbohydrates	los hidratos de carbono
fats	las grasas
proteins	las proteínas
vitamins	las vitaminas
minerals	las sales minerales

Types of food

cereals	los cereales
dairy products	los productos lácteos
drinks	las bebidas
eggs	los huevos
fats	las grasas
fish	el pescado
fruit	las frutas
meat	la carne
nuts	los frutos secos
organic food	los alimentos orgánicos
preserve (n)	la mermelada
pulses/lentils	las legumbres
sweets	los azúcares
vegetables	las hortalizas, las verduras

We have changed the ingredients in many of our products, because of the danger to health caused by fats and sweets.

Hemos cambiado los ingredientes de muchos de nuestros productos a causa del peligro para la salud que suponen las grasas y azúcares.

Parts of a meal

starter/first course	los entremeses/los entrantes [las entradas/los primeros platos]

DINING OUT, see page 27

soup	**la sopa**
salad	**la ensalada**
main course	**los platos principales**
dessert	**la postre**
cheese	**el queso**

Growing processes in food-making

to fatten	**engordar**
to fertilize	**fertilizar**
to germinate	**germinar**
to grow	**cultivar**
to harvest	**cosechar**
to hatch	**empollar**
to milk	**ordeñar**
to pick	**recolectar**
to plough/plow	**arar**
to propagate	**criar plantas**
to rear	**criar (animales)**
to slaughter	**sacrificar**
to sow	**sembrar**

We guarantee that the animals *Garantizamos que los animales*
have been organically reared and *han sido alimentados*
slaughtered in a humane way. *orgánicamente y sacrificados de*
forma indolora.

Food preparation

to bake	**hornear**
to boil	**hervir**
to chop up	**picar**
to cook	**cocinar**
to cure	**curar**
to cut	**cortar**
into pieces/slices	**en trozos/en rebanadas,**
	en rodajas
to cut up	**cortar en pedazos**
to fry	**freír**
to grill	**asar en parrilla**
to heat	**calentar**
to marinate	**marinar [adobar]**
to melt	**fundir**
to pickle	**escabechar**

to roast	asar en horno
to salt	salar
to smoke	ahumar
to stew	guisar
to sweeten	edulcorar, endulzar
to toast	tostar

We cut up the fruit into small pieces before we put it into cans. **Cortamos las frutas en pedazos pequeños antes de introducirla en atas.**

The business of catering

banquet hall	la sala de banquetes
bar	el bar
buffet	el buffet
café	el café
cafeteria	la cafetería
chef	el chef/jefe(-a) de cocina
coffeeshop	la cafetería
cook (n)	el cocinero(-a)
diner *(place)*	el restaurante económico
fast food	la comida rápida
feast	el festín, el banquete
meal	la comida
pub	el pub
refreshment	el refresco
restaurant	el restaurante
restaurateur	el dueño(-a)/el propietano(-a) del restaurante
serve	servir
teahouse	la casa de té
waiter	el camarero [el mozo, el mesero]
drinks waiter	el camarero de bebidas [el mozo/mesero de bebidas]
waitress	la camarera [la moza, la mesera]

The conference centre/center provides three main function rooms and is able to serve buffet meals for up to 300 delegates. **El centro de conferencias cuenta con tres salas principales y puede servir buffets para un máximo de 300 delegados.**

INFORMATION TECHNOLOGY

Source of information

archive	**el archivo**
databank	**el banco de datos**
database	**la base de datos**
file	**el fichero**
library	**la biblioteca**

The customer database contains the names and addresses of all our customers.

La base de datos de clientes contiene los nombres y direcciones de todos nuestros clientes.

The representation of information

digital data	**los datos digitalizados**
digitize	**digitalizar**
encipher	**codificar**
images	**las imágenes**
message	**el mensaje**
signal	**la señal**
electric signal	**la señal eléctrica**
electromagnetic signal	**la señal electromagnética**
transformation	**la transformación**

If you digitize data, you can store it in a digital form, i.e. as a series of 1s and 0s.

Si digitaliza los datos, podrá almacenarlos en forma digital, es decir como una serie de unos y ceros.

The storage of information

bit	**el bit**
byte	**el byte**
CD-ROM	**el CD-ROM**
data	**los datos**
data recording	**el registro de datos**
magnetic data recording	**el registro magnético de datos**
optical data recording	**el registro óptico de datos**
disk	**el disco**
floppy disk	**el disquete**
hard disk	**el disco duro**
compact disk	**el disco compacto**

memory	**la memoria**
random access memory (RAM)	**la memoria de acceso aleatorio (RAM)**
read-only memory (ROM)	**la memoria de sólo lectura (ROM)**

The transmission and processing of information

amplifier	**el amplificador**
computer	**el ordenador [la computadora]**
computer system	**el sistema informático [computerizado]**
computer network	**la red informática [computerizada]**
electrical impulses	**los impulsos eléctricos**
microphone	**el micrófono**
radio communication systems	**los sistemas de radiocomunicación**
radio transmitter	**el radiotransmisor**
signal	**la señal**
electronic signal	**la señal electrónica**
electromagnetic signal	**la señal electromagnética**
telephone	**el teléfono**
telephone network	**la red telefónica**
teletype networks	**las redes de teletipos**
television	**la televisión**

The new Pentium® chip is at the heart of the system, processing huge amounts of data at incredible speeds.

El nuevo chip Pentium® es la parte más importante del sistema y procesa enormes cantidades de datos a velocidades increíbles.

Processes

to convert	**convertir**
to degrade	**degradar**
to distort	**distorsionar**
to receive	**recibir**
to transmit	**transmitir**

This equipment can convert the old analog signals into digital signals.

Este equipo puede convertir las antiguas señales analógicas en señales digitales.

IT

TELECOMMUNICATIONS, see page 112

PHARMACEUTICALS AND CHEMICALS

Chemicals and life

alkaloids	los alcaloides
carbohydrates	los hidratos de carbono
cholesterol	el colesterol
coloration	la coloración
drugs	los medicamentos
enzymes	las enzimas
hormones	las hormonas
lipids	los lípidos
nucleic acids	los ácidos nucléicos
Deoxyribonucleic acid (DNA)	el ácido desoxirribonucléico (ADN)
Ribonucleic acid (RNA)	el ácido ribonucléico (ARN)
peptides	los péptidos
pigments	los pigmentos
chlorophyll	la clorofila
melanin	la melanina
proteins	las proteínas
amino acid	los aminoácidos
glutamine	la glutamina
gluten	el gluten
keratin	la queratina
myoglobin	la mioglobina
steroids	los esteroides
vitamins	las vitaminas

As the lack of any hormone may cause a major deficiency, we now synthesize most of them artificially.

Puesto que la falta de cualquier hormona puede provocar una grave deficiencia, ahora sintetizamos artificialmente la mayoría de ellas.

Body systems

autonomic nervous system	el sistema nervioso autónomo
cardiovascular system	el sistema cardiovascular
central nervous system	el sistema nervioso central
digestive system	el sistema digestivo
excretory system	el sistema excretor
histamine response system	el sistema de reacción a la histamina
immune response system	el sistema de respuesta inmune

| reproductive system | el sistema reproductor |
| skeletal muscle system | el sistema musculoesqueletal |

Our new digestive tablets help with the ingestion, digestion and absorption of food. | ***Nuestras nuevas tabletas digestivas ayudan en el proceso de ingestión, digestión y absorción de comida.***

Drugs

atropins	las atropinas
analgesics	los analgésicos
salicylic acid	el ácido salicílico
anaesthetics	los anestésicos
chloroform	el cloroformo
cocaine	la cocaína
procaine	la procaína
antibiotics	los antibióticos
penicillin	la penicilina
streptomycin	la estreptomicina
antidepressants	los antidepresivos
antiseptics	los antisépticos
beta blockers	los beta bloqueantes
chemotherapeutics	los quimioterapéuticos
quinine	la quinina
sulfa drug	la sulfamida
hallucinogens	los alucinógenos
cannabis	el canabis
hashish	el hachís
marijuana	la marihuana
mescaline	la mescalina
narcotics	los narcóticos
heroin	la heroína
methadone	la metadona
morphine	la morfina
opium	el opio
sedatives	los sedantes
barbiturates	los barbitúricos
thalidomide	la talidomidam
stimulants	los estimulantes
amphetamine	la anfetamina
caffeine	la cafeína
tranquillizers	los tranquilizantes
diazepam	el diazepán

others	otros
antacids	los antiácidos
antihistamine	el antihistamínico
diuretic	el diurético
ephedrine	la efedrina
laxative	los laxantes

Some anaesthetics are used before or during surgery to depress the central nervous system.

Algunos anestésicos se usan antes o durante la cirugía para sedar el sistema nervioso central.

The drug business

ethical drugs	los fármacos éticos
generic drugs	los fármacos genéricos
me-too products	los productos análogos
prescription drugs	los fármacos de prescripción médica [los fármacos de venta bajo receta]
proprietary/patent drugs	los fármacos patentados
veterinary pharmaceuticals	los productos farmacéuticos veterinarios

Proprietary drugs are sold over the counter; ethical drugs may be obtained legally only with a prescription from an authorized health-care provider.

Los fármacos patentados se venden sin receta médica; los fármacos éticos pueden obtenerse legalmente sólo con receta prescrita por un médico autorizado.

Drug forms

liquid	el líquido
capsule	la cápsula

Branches of medicine

clinical medicine	la medicina clínica
preventive medicine	la medicina preventiva
fringe medicine	la medicina no reconocida
alternative medicine	la medicina alternativa
complementary medicine	la medicina complementaria
holistic medicine	la medicina holística
folk medicine	el curanderismo

PROPERTY

The types of property

apartment/flat	el apartamento [el departamento]
furnished apartment	el apartamento [el departamento] amueblado
studio apartment	el estudio
apartment block/block of flats	el bloque de apartamentos [el bloque de departamentos]
bungalow	el bungalow
castle	el castillo
chalet	el chalé
consulate	el consulado
duplex/two-storey house	el dúplex
embassy	la embajada
estate	la finca [la hacienda]
farmhouse	la granja
field	el campo
grounds	los terrenos
hall	la casa solariega
house	la casa
country house	la casa de campo
ranch house	el rancho [el casco]
tenement house	la heredad
terraced (row) house	el adosado
town house	el piso
lodge	la cabaña
mansion	la mansión
office	la oficina
official residence	la residencia oficial
palace	el palacio
park	el parque
penthouse	el ático
plot	el solar
property	la propiedad
stately home	el palacete
villa	el chalé

Our client requires 350 square metres/meters of office space, fully equipped with telecommunications connections, and in a central location.

Nuestro(-a) cliente(-a) necesita una oficina de 350 metros cuadrados, totalmente equipada con conexiones de telecomunicación y en el centro de la ciudad.

CONSTRUCTION, see page 97

Property

The relationship with property

boarder	el huésped
homeowner	el propietario(-a)
householder/leaseholder	el casero(a)
lessee	el arrendatario(-a)
lessor	el arrendador(a)
lodger	el inquilino(-a)
occupier	el/la ocupante
owner	el propietario(-a)
resident	el residente
paying guest	el huésped
renter	el/la rentista
tenant	el arrendatario(-a)

Under the terms of this lease the landlord, Mr Bretón, grants possession and use of the property at this address to you as tenant or lessee for a term of 25 years.

Conforme a los términos de este contrato de arrendamiento, el propietario, Sr. Bretón, le transfiere la posesión y uso de la propiedad con esta dirección por un período de 25 años.

The legal aspects of property

assign	asignar
convey	traspasar
conveyance	el traspaso
freehold	la propiedad libre de cargas
leasehold	la propiedad arrendada
hereditament	la herencia
leasing	el arrendamiento
let/lease (v)	arrendar/alquilar
sublet/sublease (v)	subarrendar, realquilar
ownership	la propiedad
rent (v)/(n)	arrendar/la renta
rental	el arrendamiento
tenancy	el arrendamiento
tenure	la tenencia
trust, in	en administración

As a potential buyer of the freehold, it is important to check the seller's title to the property.

Como potencial comprador de una propiedad, es importante comprobar el título de propiedad del vendedor.

INDUSTRIES AND PROFESSIONS

Property

TELECOMMUNICATIONS

Systems in telecommunications

cable (n)	el cable
cablegram	el cablegrama
electronic mail	el correo electrónico
facsimile/fax	el facsímil, el fax
teleconferencing	la teleconferencia
telegamme/telegram	el telegrama
telegraphy	la telegrafía
telephony	la telefonía
videoconferencing	la videoconferencia
wire	el hilo
wireless telegraphy	la telegrafía sin hilos

Our new videoconferencing equipment allows two or more people at different locations to communicate written, spoken and visual information to each other.

Nuestro nuevo equipo de videoconferencia permite a dos o más personas de diferentes lugares comunicarse entre sí la información escrita, hablada o visual.

Technology in telecommunications

asynchronous transfer mode (ATM)	el modo de transferencia asíncrono (ATM)
bandwidth	la anchura de banda
converter	el convertidor
data	los datos
analog data	los datos analógicos
digital data	los datos digitalizados
transfer (v) data	transferir datos
modem	el módem
fax modem	el fax módem
multiplexing	la multiplexación
time-division multiplexing	la multiplexación por división del tiempo
network	la red
Internet	el Internet
local area net (LAN)	la red de área local (LAN)
wide-area networks	las redes de área extendida
signal	la señal
switching	la conmutación
packet switching	la conmutación de paquetes

The A44 modem enables computer data to be transmitted over a telephone line at very high speeds.

Nuestro módem A44 permite al ordenador transmitir datos por una línea telefónica a muy altas velocidades.

Equipment and devices in telecommunications

amplifier	el amplificador
antenna	la antena
cable	el cable
coaxial cables	los cables coaxiales
fibre/fiber optic cables	los cables de fibra óptica
circuit	el circuito
integrated circuit	el circuito integrado
printed circuit	el circuito impreso
communications satellite	las comunicaciones por satélite
electric	eléctrico(-a)
electric circuit	el circuito eléctrico
electric switch	el conmutador eléctrico
headphone	el casco telefónico
headset	el casco con auriculares
laser	el láser
loudspeaker	el altavoz [el altoparlante]
microphone	el micrófono
microprocessor	el microprocesador
microwave	la microonda
photoelectric cell	la célula fotoeléctrica
radar	el rádar
receiver	el receptor
semiconductor	el semiconductor
switchboard	el conmutador telefónico
telephone	el teléfono
car telephone	el teléfono móvil
cellular phone	el teléfono celular
radio telephone	el radioteléfono
telephone exchange	la centralita telefónica
videophone	el videteléfono
transistor	el transistor
transmitter	el transmisor

Standard coaxial cable can carry up to 132,000 messages simultaneously.

El cable coaxial estándar puede transmitir hasta 132.000 mensajes simultáneamente.

TEXTILES AND CLOTHING

Types of textiles

canvas	la lona
cashmere	el cachemir
chintz	el chintz
corduroy	la pana [el corderoy]
cotton	el algodón
damask	el damasco
denim	la tela vaquera
fibre/fiber	la fibra
flannel	la franela
gauze	la gasa
hessian	la arpillera
jute	el yute
linen	el lino
mohair	el mohair
net	el tul
satin	el satén, el raso
silk	la seda
synthetics	los tejidos sintéticos
polyester	el poliéster
polymer	el polímero
vinyl fibre/fiber	la fibra de vinilo
velvet	el terciopelo
wool	la lana

Synthetics such as nylon and polyester, which are stronger than silk and lower in price, have led to a tremendous reduction in silk production and consumption.

Los tejidos sintéticos tales como el nailon y el poliéster, que son más fuertes que la seda y más económicos, han reducido enormemente la producción y el consumo de la seda.

Processes in textile manufacture

to crochet	hacer ganchillo/crochet
to darn	zurcir
to dye	teñir
to felt	hacer fieltro
to knit	tejer, hacer punto
to press	calandrar
to twill	cruzar un tejido
to weave/spin	hilar

BANKING

The business of banking

retail banking	**la banca minorista**
wholesale/corporate banking	**la banca mayorista/corporativa**
universal/full-service banking	**la banca universal/de servicios totales**
investment banking	**la banca de inversiones**
merchant banking	**la banca de negocios**
trustee banking	**la banca fiduciaria**

We specialize in wholesale banking for corporate and institutional investors.

Nos especializamos en banca mayorista para entidades corporativas e inversores institucionales.

The services provided

account	**la cuenta**
bank account	**la cuenta bancaria**
current/checking account	**la cuenta corriente**
deposit account	**la cuenta de depósito**
savings account	**la libreta de ahorros**
time deposit account	**la cuenta de depósito a plazo**
cash dispenser/automated teller machine	**el cajero automático**
correspondent banking	**el corresponsal bancario**
credit (n)	**el crédito**
credit card	**la tarjeta de crédito**
credit limit	**el límite crediticio**
credit line	**la línea de crédito**
debit card	**la carta de débito**
deposit (n)	**el depósito**
deposit account	**la cuenta de depósito**
deposit box	**la caja de seguridad**
foreign exchange	**las divisas**
interest	**el interés**
interest rate	**el tipo de interés**
fixed interest rate	**el tipo de interés fijo**
variable interest rate	**el tipo de interés variable**
investment	**la inversión**
investment counselling	**la asesoría de inversiones**
investment services	**los servicios de inversión**

loan	el préstamo
short-term loan	el préstamo a corto plazo
long-term loan	el préstamo a largo plazo
lend	prestar
letter of credit	la carta de crédito
mortgage	la hipoteca
overdraft	el descubierto
portfolio management	la administración de títulos en cartera
project financing	la financiación de proyectos
risk analysis	el análisis de riesgos
safe-deposit box	la caja de seguridad
save	ahorrar
savings	los ahorros
transfer (n)	la transferencia
bank transfer	la transferencia bancaria
travellers' cheques/checks	los cheques de viaje

Our savings accounts offer very attractive rates of interest.

Nuestras libretas de ahorros ofrecen unos tipos de interés muy interesantes.

The profession of banking

bank manager	el director(a) [el/la gerente] de banco
cashier	el cajero(-a)
customer advisor	el asesor(a) del cliente
dealer	el/la agente
financial analyst	el/la analista financiero(-a)
financier	el financiero(-a)
investment advisor	el asesor(a) de inversiones
investment counsellor	el consejero(-a) de inversiones
investor	el inversor(a)
portfolio manager	el administrador(a) de títulos en cartera
security guard	la guarda de seguridad
teller	el cajero(-a)
trader	el/la comerciante

A portfolio manager can make day-to-day decisions about your investments.

Un administrador de títulos en cartera puede tomar las decisiones diarias sobre sus inversiones.

INSURANCE

Types of insurance

aviation insurance	el seguro aéreo
credit insurance	el seguro de riesgo de insolvencia
fire insurance	el seguro contra incendio
group insurance	el seguro colectivo
group life insurance	**el seguro de vida colectivo**
group health insurance	**el seguro de enfermedad colectivo**
group annuities	**las anualidades colectivas**
health insurance	el seguro de enfermedad
permanent health insurance	**el seguro de enfermedad permanente**
liability insurance	el seguro de responsabilidad civil
life insurance/assurance	el seguro de vida
marine insurance	el seguro marítimo
motor/car insurance	el seguro de automóviles
comprehensive	**a todo riesgo**
third party, fire and theft	**a terceros, contra incendio y robo [contra terceros, incendio y robo]**
re-insurance	el reaseguro
theft insurance	el seguro contra robos
title insurance	el seguro de invalidez de títulos sobre bienes inmuebles

Under the terms of your motor insurance, you are not covered for damage caused to your own car.

Su seguro de automóviles no cubre los daños causados a su propio coche.

Your health insurance will pay you a regular sum if you are unable to work for more than 2 months.

Su seguro de enfermedad le pagará una suma regular si no puede trabajar durante más de 2 meses.

The elements of insurance

accidental occurrence	el caso de accidente
agreement	el acuerdo
claim (n)	la reclamación,
commission	la comisión

compensation	la indemnización
contract	el contrato
hazard	el riesgo
loss	la pérdida
mutuality	la mutualidad
peril	el peligro
insurable peril	el peligro asegurable
uninsurable peril	el peligro no asegurable
policy	la póliza
cancel a policy	cancelar una póliza
issue a policy	emitir una póliza
policy coverage	la cobertura de la póliza
premium	la prima
annual premium	la prima anual
monthly premium	la prima mensual
pay a premium	pagar una prima
regular premium	la prima regular
single premium	la prima única
rating	la tarificación
reimburse	indemnizar, reembolsar
risk	el riesgo
insurable risk	el riesgo asegurable
underwriting	la suscripción
underwriting rates	las tasas de suscripción

If you want to make a claim, you must complete the form giving precise details of how the accident happened.

Si desea solicitar una indemnización deberá rellenar el formulario especificando los detalles exactos de cómo se produjo el accidente.

You can pay for your insurance by 1 annual premium or spread it over 12 monthly premiums.

Puede pagar su seguro mediante una prima anual o dividirla en 12 primas mensuales.

Risks

accident	el accidente
accidental damage	los daños por accidente
accidental loss	la pérdida accidental
breakdown	la avería
business interruption	de uso y ocupación
death	la muerte
explosion	la explosión

fire	el incendio
flood	la inundación
illness	la enfermedad

If you insure yourself against business interruption, then we will pay out in the event that you are prevented from carrying out your normal business activities. — *Si se hace un seguro de uso y ocupación, le pagaremos en el caso de que no pueda llevar a cabo sus actividades empresariales normales.*

The people involved in insurance

actuary	el actuario(-a)
adjuster	el tasador(a)
agent	el/la agente
broker	el/la agente libre
insurer	el asegurador(a)
insured	el asegurado(-a)
policy holder	el tenedor(a) de una póliza de seguros
underwriter	el suscriptor(a)

The claim

cash (n)	el efectivo
cash value	el valor en efectivo
claim damages	la reclamación por daños
compensation	la compensación, la indemnización
damages	los daños
depreciation	la depreciación
make a claim for damage	presentar una reclamación por daños
make a claim for loss	presentar una reclamación por pérdidas
new for old	el nuevo por viejo
wear and tear	el uso y desgaste

If you make a claim for damage or loss, then your compensation will be either on the basis of new for old or with a deduction for normal wear and tear. — *Si presenta una reclamación por daños o pérdidas, la compensación se calculará sobre la base de nuevo por viejo, o bien con una deducción por el uso y desgaste normales.*

LAW

General elements of law

action	el proceso judicial
bring an action against someone	incoar un proceso judicial contra alguien
award (n)/(v)	el laudo/ajudicar
capacity	la capacidad
case	la causa
civil case	la causa civil
criminal case	la causa penal
claim (n)	la demanda
make a claim against someone	presentar una demanda contra alguien
compensation	la compensación
court	el tribunal
take someone to court	llevar a alguien a los tribunales
damage	el daño
damages	los daños
defendant	el defensor(a)
dispute (n)	el litigio
settle a dispute	resolver un litigio
duty	la obligación
duty of care	la obligación de cuidados
impose a duty	imponer una obligación
fine (n)	la multa
gross (adj)	grave
gross incompetence	la incompetencia grave
gross misconduct	la conducta impropia grave
gross negligence	la imprudencia temeraria
grounds	los motivos
judge (n)	el juez
law	la lay, el derecho
lawyer	el abogado(-a)
legislation	la legislación
liability	la responsabilidad
offence	el delito
offend	ofender
offender	el ofensor(a)
party	la parte
guilty party	la parte culpable
responsible party	la parte responsable
plaintiff	el/la demandante

LEGAL DEPARTMENT, see page 78

prison	el/la cárcel
imprisonment	el encarcelamiento
proceedings	los procedimientos
prosecute	procesar
remedy (n)	el recurso
sentence (n)	la sentencia
sue	demandar
terms/requirements	las condiciones
title	el título
valid	válido(-a)
invalid	inválido(-a)
validity	la validez

Contract law

accept	aceptar
acceptance	la aceptación
agreement	el contrato
conditions of an agreement	las condiciones de un contrato
terms of an agreement	los términos de un contrato
bid (n)	la propuesta
breach (v)	incumplir
breach of contract	el incumplimiento de contrato
clause	la cláusula
compensation	la compensación, la indemnización
consideration	la causa
contract (n)	el contrato
break a contract	romper un contrato
enter into a contract	firmar un contrato
make a contract	celebrar un contrato
oral contract	el contrato verbal
rescind a contract	rescindir un contrato
terminate a contract	terminar un contrato
written contract	el contrato (por) escrito
intention to create legal relations	la intención de crear relaciones legales
offer (n)	la oferta
make an offer	presentar una oferta
withdraw an offer	retirar una oferta
party	la parte
sue	demandar

LEGAL ASPECTS OF NEGOTIATIONS, see page 55

Law

Employment law

discriminate	discriminar
discriminate against someone on the basis of sex, race or religion	discriminar a alguien por razones de sexo, raza o religión
dismiss	despedir
dismissal	el despido
fire (v)	despedir
lump sum	a tanto alzado
misconduct	la conducta impropia
pension	la pensión
pensionable age	la edad de jubilación
pension off	jubilar
re-engage	renovar
re-engagement	la renovación
redundant/laid off	despedido(-a) por reducción de plantilla
make someone redundant/lay someone off	despedir a alguien por reducción de plantilla
redundancy/dismissal payment	la indemnización por reducción de plantilla
reinstate	reincorporar
reinstatement	la reincorporación
retire	retirar
retirement	el retiro
sack (v)	despedir
strike (n)	la huelga
trade union	el sindicato

If you are in breach of the terms of your contract of employment, you can be dismissed. — *Si incumple alguno de los términos de su contrato laboral puede ser despedido.*

Civil law

arbitrate	arbitrar
arbitration	el arbitraje
conveyancing	los traspaso
damages	la daños
claim (n) for damages	la reclamación por daños
liable	responsable
litigate	litigar
litigation	el litigio
statute	el estatuto

PERSONNEL DEPARTMENT, see page 86

TOURISM AND LEISURE

Outdoor leisure activities

archery	el tiro con arco
bobsleighing/bobsledding	el bobsleigh
camping	el camping
caving	la espeleología
curling	el curling
cycling	el ciclismo
diving	el submarinismo
deep-sea diving	el submarinismo a grandes profundidades
skin diving	el buceo
exploring	la exploración
flying	el vuelo
gliding	el vuelo sin motor [el planeo]
hang gliding	el vuelo con ala delta
paragliding	el parapente
hiking	el senderismo
hunting	la caza
jogging	el jogging
luging	la vela
mountaineering	el montañismo
orienteering	la orientación
riding	la equitación
rock-climbing	el alpinismo
shooting	el tiro
skating	el patinaje
ice hockey	el hockey sobre hielo
ice skating	el patinaje sobre hielo
skiing	el esquí
downhill skiing	el esquí de descenso
cross-country skiing	el esquí de fondo
langlauf	la carrera de fondo
ski-jumping	los saltos de esquí
water skiing	el esquí acuático
snorkling	el buceo con tubo de respiración
surfing	el surfing
wind-surfing	el windsurfing
swimming	la natación
tobogganing	deslizarse en tobogán
walking	la marcha

weight-training	la halterofilia
weightlifting	el levantamiento de pesas

Many people now take two holidays/vacations a year: a skiing holiday/vacation in winter and a beach holiday/vacation in summer.

Muchos dividen sus vacaciones en dos veces al año: vacaciones para esquiar en invierno y vacaciones en la playa en verano.

Travel and Tourism

biking	el paseo en bicicleta
bus tour	el viaje en autobús
business trip	el viaje de negocios
cruise	el crucero
cycling	los recorridos en bicicleta
driving	el viaje en coche
excursion	la excursión
expedition	la expedición
grand tour	la gran gira, el gran tour
hiking	la marcha
joy ride	el paseo en coche
motoring	el automovilismo
outing	las salidas al campo
package tour	el viaje organizado
pleasure trip	el viaje de placer
ramble (n)	la vuelta
ride (v)	montar
riding	la equitación
safari	el safari
shopping	las compras
study holiday/vacation	las vacaciones de estudio
tour/journey	el viaje
package tour	el viaje organizado
trek (n)	la caminata
trip	el viaje
visit (n)	la visita
voyage (n)	la travesía
walking	el paseo

Meditours are offering an autumn cruise around the Mediterranean.

La agencia de viaje está ofreciendo un crucero por el Mediterráneo para otoño.

English–Spanish Business Dictionary

f	**feminine**
m	**masculine**
pl	**plural**
(adj)	**adjective**
(adv)	**adverb**
(n)	**noun**
(v)	**verb**
so.	**someone**
sth.	**something**

A

abandon an action
desistir de una acción
abroad en el extranjero
absent ausente
absolute monopoly
monopolio *m* absoluto
accept (v) aceptar
accept delivery of a shipment
aceptar la entrega de mercancías
accept liability for sth. aceptar la
responsabilidad de algo
acceptable aceptable, admisible
acceptance aceptación *f*
account cuenta *f*
account for justificar, responder de
account in credit cuenta *f* con
saldo positivo
account, on a crédito
account on stop cuenta *f*
bloqueada
accountant contable *m*
accounts contabilidad *f*
accounts department
departamento *m* de contabilidad
accounts payable
cuentas *fpl* a/por pagar
accounts receivable cuentas *fpl*
a/por cobrar
accrue acumularse, devengar
accused acusado(-a)
acknowledge receipt of a letter
acusar recibo de una carta
acquire adquirir
acquisition adquisición *f*, compra *f*
across-the-board general
act of God fuerza *f* mayor

acting manager director *m*
en funciones
action for damages demanda *f* por
daños y perjuicios
activity actividad *f*
actuals cifras *fpl* reales
add on 10% for service añadir el 10%
por el servicio
additional charges
cargos *mpl* adicionales
additional premium sobreprima *f*
address (n) dirección *f*, señas *fpl*
address *(letter, parcel)* dirigir a
adjourn a meeting aplazar una reunión
adjudication tribunal
tribunal *m* de justicia
adjustment ajuste *m*, reajuste *m*
administration administración *f*
administrative staff
personal *m* administrativo
admission charge precio *m* de entrada
advance (n) *(loan)* anticipo *m*
advance (v) *(lend)* anticipar
advance booking reserva *f* anticipada
advance on account anticipo *m* a cuenta
advance payment pago *m* anticipado
advantage of, take aprovechar(se)
advertise anunciar
advertisement anuncio *m*
advertiser anunciante *m/f*
advertising agency agencia *f*
de publicidad
advertising budget presupuesto *m*
de publicidad
advertising rates tarifas *fpl* publicitarias
advertising space
espacio *m* publicitario
advice note nota *f* de aviso
advise aconsejar
after-sales service
servicio *m* posventa
after-tax profit
beneficios *mpl* netos de impuestos
agency agencia *f*
agenda orden *m* del día
agent *(rep)* representante *m/f*
agree *(approve)* aprobar, acordar,
convenir; *(be same as)*
corresponder, coincidir
agree to do sth. aceptar hacer algo

agreed price
  precio m acordado, convenido

agreement convenio m, acuerdo m

aim (n) objetivo m, propósito m

aim (v) proponerse, aspirar a

air freight flete m aéreo,
  carga f aérea

air freight charges/rates tarifas de
  carga aérea

airfreight (v) enviar por carga aérea

airmail (n) correo m aéreo

airmail (v) enviar por correo aéreo

airport aeropuerto m

airtight packaging
  embalaje m hermético

all expenses paid todos los
  gastos pagados

all-in price precio m todo incluido

all-risks policy póliza f a todo riesgo

allow 10% for carriage dejar un
  margen del 10% para el porte

allowance for depreciation cuota f
  de depreciación

alter cambiar

amend enmendar

amendment enmienda f

amortization amortización f

amortize amortizar

amount (of money) importe m;
  (quantity) cantidad f

amount owing importe m debido

amount paid importe m pagado

amount to ascender a

analysis análisis m

annual accounts cuentas fpl anuales

annual general meeting junta f
  general anual

annual report informe m anual

annually anualmente

answer (n) respuesta f,
  contestación f; (v) responder,
  contestar

answer the telephone contestar
  el teléfono

answering machine
  contestador m automático

appeal (against a decision) (n)
  apelación f; (v) apelar

appeal to (v) (attract) atraer, interesar

appendix anexo m

application aplicación f, solicitud f

application form impreso m/
  formulario m de solicitud

apply for a job solicitar un trabajo

apply to (affect) referirse (a)

appoint nombrar

appointment (job) empleo m;
  (meeting) cita f, compromiso m

appointments book agenda f

appointments vacant ofertas fpl
  de trabajo

appreciate apreciar

appreciation apreciación f

approval, on a prueba

approve the terms of a contract
  aprobar los términos de un
  contrato

approximate aproximado(-a)

approximately aproximadamente

arbitrate in a dispute arbitrar un
  litigio/en una disputa

arbitration board/tribunal
  comisión f/ tribunal m de arbitraje

area code código m postal/territorial

area manager director(a) regional

arrange (meeting) organizar

arrears atrasos mpl

article (clause) cláusula f;
  (item) artículo m

as per advice
  según nota de expedición

as per invoice según factura

as per sample según muestra

ask (question) preguntar;
  (so. to do sth.) pedir

ask for a refund exigir el reembolso

ask for further details
  pedir más detalles

assess damages fijar los daños

assessment of damages valoración f
  de daños

asset activo m

asset value valor m de activo

assist ayudar, asistir

assistant ayudante m/f, auxiliar m/f,
  adjunto(-a)

assistant manager subdirector(a)

associate (adj) asociado(-a),
  afiliado(-a); (n) socio(-a)

assurance seguro m

assurance policy póliza f de seguros

assure so.'s life asegurar la vida
  de alguien

attend (meeting) asistir

attention atención f

attractive salary salario m interesante

auction (n) subasta f
auction (v) subastar
audit (n) auditoría f, revisión f
de cuentas
audit the accounts revisar las cuentas
auditor censor(a),
interventor(a), auditor(a)
authority autoridad f
authorization autorización f
authorize payment autorizar el pago
availability disponibilidad f
available disponible, accesible
average (adj) medio(-a), mediano(-a)
average (n) *(insurance)* avería f
average price precio m
medio/corriente
await instructions
esperar instrucciones
award a contract to so. adjudicar un
contrato a alguien

B

back orders pedidos *mpl* pendientes
back tax impuesto m atrasado
back up (v) *(computer file)* archivar;
(support) respaldar, apoyar
backdate antedatar
backlog
acumulación f de trabajo atrasado
backup copy copia f de reserva/
de seguridad
bad debt deuda f morosa/incobrable
balance (n) saldo m, balance m
balance (v) *(a budget)*
equilibrar, saldar
**balance carried down/carried
forward** saldo m a cuenta nueva
balance due to us saldo m deudor,
saldo a (nuestro) favor
balance of payments balanza f
de pagos
balance of trade balanza f comercial
balance sheet balance m general/
de situación
ban (n) prohibición f
ban (v) prohibir
bank (n) banco m
bank (v) ingresar, depositar
bank account cuenta f bancaria
bank balance estado m de cuenta
bank base rate tipo m base de
interés bancario

bank charges gastos *mpl* bancarios
bank draft giro m bancario
bank holiday fiesta f oficial
bank statement extracto m
de cuentas
bank transfer
transferencia f bancaria
banker's order orden f de
domiciliación (bancaria)
banknote billete m de banco
bankrupt (adj)/(n) insolvente,
quebrado(-a); (v) arruinar
bankruptcy insolvencia f,
quiebra f, bancarrota f
bar chart gráfico m de barras
bar code código m de barras
bargain (n) ganga f; *(deal)* negocio m
bargain (v) regatear, negociar
bargaining position
postura f negociadora
barter (n) trueque m; (v) trocar
base (n) base f
basic (adj) fundamental
basic discount descuento m básico
basic tax impuesto m básico
batch (n) *(of products)* lote m
batch (v) agrupar
batch number número m de lote
bear (v) *(interest)* devengar, rendir
bearer portador(a)
bearer bond título m al portador
begin empezar, comenzar
behalf of, on en nombre de
benchmark punto m de referencia
beneficiary beneficiario(-a)
benefit from (v) beneficiarse de
berth (v) atracar
bid (n) *(offer to buy)* oferta f
bilateral bilateral
bill (n) *(in a restaurant)* cuenta f; *(list
of charges)* factura f
bill (v) facturar
bill of exchange letra f de cambio
bill of lading
conocimiento m de embarque
bill of sale contrato m de venta
bills payable/receivable cuentas *fpl*/
letras *fpl* a pagar/cobrar
black market mercado m negro
blacklist (v) poner en la lista negra
blank cheque/check cheque m
en blanco
block (v) bloquear

block booking

block booking reserva *f* en bloque
board (n) *(group)* consejo *m*
board (v) abordar, embarcarse
board meeting reunión *f* del consejo de administración
board of directors junta *f* directiva
bond *(government)* bono *m*, título *m*
bonus prima *f*, bonificación *f*
book (v) reservar
book value valor *m* contable
bookkeeper contable *m/f*
bookkeeping contabilidad *f*
border frontera *f*
borrow pedir/tomar prestado
borrower prestatario(-a)
boss amo *m*, jefe(-a)
bottleneck atasco *m*, embotellamiento *m*
bought ledger libro *m* mayor de compras
bounce *(cheque/check)* devolver por falta de fondos
box number (número de) apartado *m* de correos
bracket together agrupar
branch sucursal *f*
brand marca *f*
brand loyalty fidelidad *f* a la marca
brand name marca *f* comercial
breach of contract violación *f* de contrato
break an agreement romper un acuerdo
break down (v) *(itemize)* desglosar, detallar; *(machine)* estropearse, averiarse
break even (v) cubrir gastos
break off negotiations romper las negociaciones
break the law infringir la ley
breakdown (n) *(items)* desglose *m*, detalle *m*; *(machine)* avería *f*
breakeven point punto *m* muerto
bribe (n) soborno *m*
bribe (v) sobornar
briefcase cartera *f*, maletín *m*
brochure folleto *m* publicitario
budget (n) presupuesto *m*; (v) presupuestar
budget account *(in bank)* cuenta *f* presupuestaria
budgetary control control *m* presupuestario

built-in incorporado(-a)
bulk buying compra *f* a granel
bureau de change agencia *f* de cambio
business *(commerce)* comercio *m*, negocios *mpl*; *(company)* empresa *f*
business, on por asuntos de negocios
business address dirección *f* comercial
business class clase *f* preferente
business hours horas *fpl* de oficina
business lunch almuerzo *m* de negocios
business premises local *m* comercial
business school escuela *f* de empresariales
business strategy estrategia *f* comercial
businessman/businesswoman hombre *m*/mujer *f* de negocios
busy ocupado(-a)
buy (v) comprar, adquirir
buy forward comprar a futuros
buyer *(person)* comprador(a)
buying department sección *f* de compras

C

calculate calcular
calculation cálculo *m*
calculator calculadora *f*
calendar calendario *m*
calendar month mes *m* civil
calendar year año *m* civil
call (n) *(phone)* llamada *f*; *(visit)* visita *f*
call (v) *(phone)* llamar
call off a deal suspender/anular un acuerdo
cancel cancelar, suspender, anular
cancel a contract rescindir/anular un contrato
cancellation clause cláusula *f* de rescisión
cancellation of an appointment cancelación *f* de una cita
capacity capacidad *f*; *(ability)* aptitud *f*, habilidad *f*; *(production)* rendimiento *m*
capital capital *m*

capital expenditure gastos *mpl* de capital
capital gains plusvalía *f*
capitalization capitalización *f*
capitalize capitalizar
capitalize on aprovechar
captive market mercado *m* cautivo
capture acaparar
card *(business card)* tarjeta *f*
card index (n)
fichero *m*, clasificador *m*
card phone teléfono *m* de tarjeta
cardboard box caja *f* de cartón
care of (c/o) para entregar a
cargo carga *f*
carriage porte *m*, transporte *m*
carriage forward porte *m* debido
carriage free franco de porte
carriage paid porte *m* pagado, franco a domicilio
carrier *(person)* transportista *m/f*; *(company)* empresa *f* de transportes
carry *(in stock)* tener en existencia; *(transport)* llevar, transportar
carry forward pasar a cuenta nueva
carry on a business llevar un negocio
carton *(box)* caja *f* de cartón
case (n) *(box)* caja *f*
cash (n) *(money)* dinero *m* efectivo
cash a cheque/check
cobrar un cheque
cash advance anticipo *m* de caja a cuenta
cash balance saldo *m* de caja
cash book libro *m* de caja
cash card
tarjeta *f* de cajero automático
cash desk caja *f*
cash discount
descuento *m* por pago al contado
cash dispenser cajero *m* automático
cash float fondo *m* de caja
cash flow flujo *m* de caja, 'cash flow' *m*
cash flow forecast previsión *f* de 'cash flow'
cash offer oferta *f* en metálico
cash on delivery (c.o.d.) cobro *m* a la entrega/contra reembolso
cash payment pago *m* al contado
cash price precio *m* al contado
cash purchase compra *f* al contado

cash sale venta *f* al contado
cashier cajero(-a)
casting vote voto *m* de calidad
casual work trabajo *m* eventual
catalogue/catalog catálogo *m*
category categoría *f*
cater for atender a, abastecer
caveat emptor por cuenta y riesgo del comprador
ceiling price precio *m* tope, precio máximo autorizado
cellular telephone teléfono *m* celular/móvil
central bank banco *m* central
central purchasing centralización *f* de las compras
centralize centralizar
certificate of approval certificado *m* de aprobación
certificate of origin
certificado *m* de origen
certified cheque/check
cheque *m* conformado
certified copy
compulsa *f*, copia *f* certificada
certify certificar
chain (of stores) cadena *f*
chairman *(company)* presidente(-a)
chairman and managing director
presidente y director gerente
Chamber of Commerce Cámara *f* de Comercio
change (n) *(cash)* cambio *m*, dinero *m* suelto; *(difference)* vuelta *f*
change (v) cambiar
change hands cambiar de dueño
channels of distribution canales *mpl* de distribución
charge (n) *(money)* precio *m*, cargo *m*, gastos *mpl*
charge (v) *(money)* cobrar
charge a purchase cargar una compra en cuenta
charge card tarjeta *f* de crédito
charter flight vuelo *m* chárter
chase *(an order)* apremiar, perseguir
cheap barato(-a)
cheap rate tarifa *f* reducida
check (n) *(examination)*
control *m*, comprobación *f*
check (v) *(examine)*
comprobar, cotejar

check in

check in *(at airport)* presentarse, facturar el equipaje
check in *(at hotel)* registrarse
check-in *(at hotel)* recepción *f*
check-in (counter) *(airport)* mostrador *m* de facturación
check-in time horario *m* de presentación en el aeropuerto
check out *(of hotel)* pagar la cuenta y marcharse
check sample muestra *f* de prueba
checkout *(in supermarket)* caja *f*
cheque/check cheque *m*
cheque/check book talonario *m* de cheques
chief *(adj)* principal
chief executive officer (CEO) jefe *m* ejecutivo, director(a) general
choice *(n) (of items)* surtido *m*
choose elegir
Christmas bonus paga *f* extraordinaria de Navidad
circular *(n)* circular *f*
circular letter of credit carta *f* de crédito general
claim *(n)* reivindicación *f*, reclamación *f*, demanda *f*
claim *(v) (insurance)* exigir, reivindicar, reclamar
claims department departamento *m* de reclamaciones
class categoría *f*, clase *m*
classified advertisements anuncios *mpl* por palabras
classified directory directorio *m* comercial, guía *f* alfabética
classify clasificar
clause cláusula *f*
clear *(adj) (understandable)* claro(-a)
clear *(v) (stock)* liquidar existencias
clear a cheque/check tramitar el pago de un cheque
clear profit ganancia *f* neta
clearing bank banco *m* comercial
clerical error error *m* de copia, error de oficina
clerk oficinista *m/f*
client cliente *m/f*
clientele clientela *f*
clinch (a deal) cerrar (un trato)
close *(a meeting)* clausurar, levantar una sesión
close an account cerrar una cuenta

close down cerrar
closed cerrado(-a)
closing *(n)* cierre *m*
closing balance saldo *m* final
closing date fecha *f* tope, fecha límite
closing price precio *m* al cierre
closing stock existencias *fpl* finales
closing time hora *f* de cierre
co-operate cooperar
co-operation cooperación *f*
co-opt so. nombrar por coopción
code of practice normas *fpl* de conducta
coin moneda *f*
cold call visita *f* comercial sin cita previa
cold store almacén *m* frigorífico
collaborate colaborar
collaboration colaboración *f*
collapse *(n)* derrumbamiento *m*, hundimiento *m*
collapse *(v)* hundirse, derrumbarse
collateral *(n)* garantía *f*
collect *(v) (fetch)* recoger
collect a debt cobrar una deuda
collect call llamada *f* a cobro revertido
collection *(of goods)* recogida *f*
collective ownership propiedad *f* colectiva
collector cobrador(a), recaudador(a)
commerce comercio *m*
commercial *(adj)* comercial; *(n) (TV)* emisión *f* publicitaria, anuncio *m*
commercial law derecho *m* mercantil
commission *(money)* comisión *f*
commission rep representante *m/f* a comisión
commit funds to a project asignar fondos a un proyecto
commitments compromisos *mpl*
commodity mercancía *f*, producto *m*
commodity exchange lonja *f*/bolsa *f* de contratación
commodity market lonja *f*/bolsa *f* de comercio
common común
common pricing fijación *f* colectiva de precios
communicate comunicar(se)
communications comunicaciones *fpl*

commute *(travel)* viajar diariamente al trabajo
commuter viajero(-a) diario(-a)
company compañía f, sociedad f
company director director(a) de una empresa
comparable comparable
compare comparar, cotejar
compare prices comparar precios
compare with comparar con
comparison comparación f
compensate compensar, indemnizar
compensation compensación f, indemnización f
competing (adj) competitivo(-a)
competition competencia f
competitive price precio m competitivo
competitiveness competitividad f
competitor competidor(a)
complain (about) quejarse
complaint queja f
complaints department oficina f de reclamaciones
complete (adj) completo(-a)
complete (v) completar, concluir, acabar
complimentary ticket entrada f de favor
comply with obedecer
compound interest interés m compuesto
comprehensive insurance seguro m a todo riesgo
compromise (n) conciliación f, acuerdo m
compromise (v) transigir
compulsory obligatorio(-a)
compulsory purchase expropiación f forzosa
computer ordenador m
computer error error m de ordenador
computer file archivo m, fichero m
computer printout copia f impresa
computer program programa m de ordenador
computer services servicios mpl de informática
computer system sistema m informático

computerize informatizar
concern (n) *(worry)* preocupación f, inquietud f
concern (v) *(deal with)* ocuparse de, referirse
conclude *(agreement)* concluir
conclusion conclusión f
condition condición f
condition that, on a condición de que
conditional condicional
conditions of employment condiciones fpl de empleo
conditions of sale condiciones fpl de venta
conduct negotiations llevar negociaciones
conference room sala f de juntas/de conferencias
confidential confidencial
confirm a booking confirmar una reserva
confirmation confirmación f
conflict of interest conflicto m de intereses
connecting flight vuelo m de correspondencia
connection vínculo m, relación f
consignment *(sending)* consignación f, envío m, expedición f; *(things sent)* envío m, remesa f
consignment note nota f de expedición/envío
consist of constar de
consolidate *(shipments)* agrupar
consortium consorcio m
constant constante, invariable
consult consultar
consultancy firm asesoría f, consultoría f
consultant asesor(a), consejero(-a)
consumer consumidor(a)
consumer goods bienes mpl de consumo
consumer price index índice m de precios al consumo (IPC)
consumer research investigación f sobre el consumo
contact (n) *(person)* contacto m, enchufe m
contact (v) contactar
contain contener

container (box, tin) recipiente m,
envase m; (shipping)
contenedor m

container terminal
terminal f de contenedores

contents contenido m

contingency plan
plan m de emergencia

continual continuo(-a)

continually continuamente

continue continuar, proseguir

continuous continuo(-a)

contra account cuenta f compensada

contra an entry anotar una
contrapartida/un contrasiento

contra entry
contrapartida f, contraasiento m

contract (n) contrato m

contract (v) contratar

contract note contrato m de Bolsa

contract of employment contrato m
de empleo

contractor contratista m/f

contractual liability
responsabilidad f contractual

contractually según, por contrato

contrary contrario(-a)

control (n) control m, mando m

control a business
controlar/dirigir un negocio

convene convocar

convenient cómodo(-a), conveniente

conversion price/rate precio m/tasa f
de conversión

convert convertir, cambiar, apropiar

convertible loan stock valores mpl
convertibles en acciones

copy (n) (of document) copia f

copy (v) copiar

corner the market
acaparar el mercado

corporate image imagen f pública de
una empresa

corporate plan plan m de trabajo de
una empresa

corporate profits beneficios mpl de
la empresa

corporation
corporación f, sociedad f mercantil

corporation tax impuesto m
de sociedades

correct (adj) correcto(-a)

correct (v) corregir

correspond with so.
escribir a alguien

correspond with sth.
corresponder a algo

correspondence correspondencia f

cost (n) costo m, coste m

cost (v) costar, valer

cost analysis análisis m de costes

cost centre/center centro m de costes

cost, insurance and freight (c.i.f.)
coste, seguro y flete, cif

cost of living carestía f, coste m
de vida

cost of sales coste m de ventas

cost plus costo m más honorarios,
porcentaje m de comisión

cost price precio m de coste

cost-effective
beneficioso (-a), rentable

cost-effectiveness rentabilidad f

cost-of-living index índice m del
coste de vida

costs costas fpl

counter mostrador m, ventanilla f

counter-claim (n) reconvención f

counter-claim (v)
presentar una reconvención

counter-offer contraoferta f

counterfoil comprobante m, matriz f
(de un talonario)

countermand revocar, cancelar

countersign refrendar

country of origin
país m de origen

coupon ad cupón m de anuncio

courier (guide) guía m/f de turismo;
(messenger) mensajero(-a)

court audiencia f,
tribunal m, juzgado m

cover (n) (insurance) garantía f,
cobertura f; (top) cubierta f, funda f

cover a risk cubrir un riesgo

cover (v) **costs** cubrir gastos

cover note póliza f provisional, nota f
de cobertura

covering letter
carta f adjunta/ explicatoria

credit (n) crédito m

credit (v) abonar, acreditar

credit account cuenta f de crédito

credit balance haber m, saldo m
acreedor/a favor

credit card sale venta *f* con tarjeta de crédito
credit control control *m* de crédito
credit entry abono *m*
credit freeze congelación *f* de créditos
credit limit límite *m* de crédito
credit note nota *f* de abono, nota *f* de crédito
credit side haber *m*
credit, on a crédito
creditor acreedor(-a)
cumulative acumulativo(-a)
currency moneda *f*
current account cuenta *f* corriente
current assets activo *m* circulante
current liabilities pasivo *m* circulante, obligaciones *fpl* a corto plazo
current rate of exchange tipo *m* de cambio actual
curriculum vitae (CV) curriculum (vitae) *m*
customer cliente *m/f*
customer satisfaction satisfacción *f* del cliente
customer service department servicio *m* de atención al cliente
customs aduana *f*
customs clearance despacho *m* aduanero/de aduanas
customs declaration form impreso *m* de declaración de aduana
customs entry point puesto *m* aduanero
customs examination inspección *f* aduanera
customs official aduanero(-a), funcionario(-a) de aduanas
cut (n) recorte *m*, rebaja *f*
cut (v) rebajar, recortar
cut price (n) precio *m* reducido
cut-price goods mercancías *fpl* a precio reducido
cycle ciclo *m*
cyclical factors factores *mpl* cíclicos

D

damage (n) daño *m*
damage (v) dañar
damages daños *mpl* y perjuicios
dangerous peligroso(-a)
data datos *mpl*

database base *f* de datos
date (n) fecha *f*; (v) fechar
date stamp fechador *m*
day día *m*
dead account cuenta *f* inactiva
dead loss siniestro *m*/pérdida *f* total
deadline fecha *f* límite, plazo *m*, límite *m*
deadlock (n) punto *m* muerto
deadlock (v) estar en punto muerto
deal (n) negocio *m*, acuerdo *m*, trato *m*
deal in (v) comerciar, tratar en
deal with an order servir/despachar un pedido
dealer comerciante *m/f*, tratante *m/f*
dear caro(-a), costoso(-a)
debenture bono *m*, pagaré *m*, obligación *f*
debit (n) débito *m*, debe *m*
debit an account adeudar/cargar en cuenta
debit entry asiento *m* de débito/adeudo
debit note nota *f* de adeudo
debt deuda *f*
debt collection cobro *m* de morosos
debtor deudor(-a), prestatario(-a)
decide decidir; *(on a course of action)* optar
deciding factor factor *m* decisivo
decimal point coma *f*/punto *m* decimal
declare goods to customs declarar mercancías en la aduana
declared value valor *m* declarado
decrease (n) descenso *m*, reducción *f*
decrease (v) disminuir, bajar, reducir
decrease in value disminución *f* de valor
decreasing (adj) decreciente
deduct deducir, descontar
deductible deducible
deduction deducción *f*
deed título *m*, escritura *f*
default (n) incumplimiento *m*, falta *f*
default on payments incumplir los pagos
defaulter moroso(-a), deudor(a)
defect defecto *m*, tara *f*
defective *(faulty)* defectuoso(-a)
defer payment diferir el pago

deferment of payment
aplazamiento m de pago
deferred creditor
acreedor(a) diferido(-a)
deficit déficit m
deficit financing financiación f del
déficit presupuestario
defray (costs) pagar, sufragar
delay (n) demora f, retraso m
delay (v) demorar, retrasar
delegate delegado(-a)
delete suprimir
deliver entregar, repartir
delivered price precio m de entrega
delivery (goods) entrega f
delivery date fecha f de entrega
delivery note albarán m
delivery time plazo m de entrega
demand (n) (for payment)
reclamación f, requerimiento m de
pago; (need) demanda f
demand (v) exigir, reclamar
demonstrate demostrar, mostrar
demonstration model modelo m
de prueba
department
departamento m, sección f
depend on depender de
depending on según
deposit (n) (in bank) depósito m,
ingreso m, imposición f; (paid in
advance) depósito, señal f,
entrada f
deposit (v) depositar, ingresar
deposit account cuenta f de
depósito, cuenta a plazo
deposit slip
nota f/recibo m de depósito
depositor
depositante m/f, impositor(a)
depreciate (lose value) depreciarse,
perder valor
depreciation (loss of value)
depreciación f, pérdida f de valor
depreciation rate coeficiente m/tasa f
de amortización
deputize for so. sustituir a alguien
deputy delegado(-a),
adjunto(-a), suplente m/f
deputy managing director director m
general adjunto
design (n) diseño m
design (v) diseñar, proyectar

design department departamento m
de diseño
desk escritorio m,
mesa f de despacho
destination destino m
detail (n) detalle m
detailed account
cuenta f/factura f detallada
devaluation
devaluación f, desvalorización f
devalue devaluar, desvalorizar
develop desarrollar
development desarrollo m
diagram diagrama m, gráfico m
dial a number marcar un número
dialling code prefijo m
differ diferir, ser distinto
differences in price diferencias fpl
de precio
direct (adj) directo(-a)
direct (v) dirigir
direct debit
domiciliación f bancaria
direct mail venta f por correo
direct tax impuesto m directo
direct-mail advertising publicidad f
por correo
directions for use instrucciones fpl
director director(a), consejero(-a)
directory
guía f, anuario m, directorio m
disclaimer renuncia f, abandono m
de responsabilidad
disclosure revelación f
discontinue suspender, interrumpir
discount (n)
descuento m, bonificación f
discount (v) descontar
discount price
precio m con descuento
discounted cash flow (DCF) cash
flow actualizado, flujo de caja
descontado
discrepancy
discrepancia f, diferencia f
discuss discutir
discussion discusión f, debate m
disk disco m
disk drive disquetera f
dismiss despedir
dismissal despido m
dispatch (n) (sending)
despacho m, envío m

dispatch (v) *(send)* enviar, consignar, despachar, expedir
dispatch note nota f de expedición/ de envío
display (n) exposición f, exhibición f
display (v) exhibir, exponer
display material material m de exposición
display stand estantería f, vitrina f de exposición
disposable desechable, de usar y tirar
disposal venta f
dispose of sth. deshacerse de algo
distribute *(goods)* distribuir, repartir
distribution distribución f, reparto m
distribution costs costes mpl de distribución
distribution manager jefe(-a) de distribución
distributor distribuidor(a)
diversification diversificación f
diversify diversificar
dividend dividendo m
dividend yield rentabilidad f del dividendo
division *(part of a company)* departamento m, sección f, rama f
do business hacer negocios
dock (n) muelle m, dique m
dock (v) *(ship)* entrar en dársena, atracar
document documento m
documentation documentación f
dollar dólar m
dollar balance reserva f en dólares
domestic market mercado m interior/nacional
domestic production producción f interior/nacional
domestic sales ventas fpl nacionales
door-to-door de puerta en puerta
door-to-door selling venta f a domicilio
dossier expediente m
double (v) duplicar(se)
double taxation doble imposición f
double-booking doble reserva f
down payment entrada f, depósito m, pago m inicial
down-market dirigido(-a) a un mercado popular
downside factor factor m de riesgo

downtown (adv) en el centro de la ciudad, hacia el centro
downturn descenso m
draft (n) *(money)* letra f, giro m; *(plan)* borrador m, proyecto m
draft a contract redactar un contrato
draft plan anteproyecto m
draw *(a cheque/check)* girar
draw up *(a contract)* preparar, redactar
drawee librado(-a)
drawer librador(a)
drop (n) caída f, baja f
drop (v) descender, bajar, caer
drop in sales caída f de las ventas
due *(awaited)* que está por llegar; *(owing)* debido(-a), vencido(-a)
dues pedidos mpl por servir
dummy producto m ficticio
dummy pack embalaje vacío/ficticio
dump goods on a market practicar el 'dumping'
duplicate (n) duplicado m, copia f
duplicate (v) copiar, duplicar
duration duración f
duty *(tax)* impuestos mpl, arancel m
duty-free libre de impuestos

E

earmark funds for a project asignar fondos a un proyecto
earn *(interest)* devengar; *(money)* ganar
earnings *(profit)* ganancias f, beneficios m; *(salary)* ingresos m
easy terms facilidades fpl de pago
economic cycle ciclo m económico
economic development desarrollo m económico
economic growth crecimiento m económico
economic trends tendencias fpl económicas
economical económico(-a)
economies of scale economías fpl de escala
economize economizar
economy economía f
economy class clase económica/ turista
ecu/ECU (European currency unit) ecu, ECU m

effect

effect (n) efecto m
effect (v) efectuar
effective yield
rendimiento m efectivo
effectiveness eficiencia f, eficacia f
efficiency eficiencia f, eficacia f
efficient eficaz, eficiente
electronic mail (e-mail)
correo m electrónico
electronic point of sale (EPOS)
puntos mpl de venta electrónicos
embargo (n) embargo m, prohibición f; (v) prohibir, embargar
embark embarcar
embark on embarcarse en
employ emplear
employee empleado(-a)
employer empresario(-a)
employment empleo m
empty (adj) vacío(-a)
enclose adjuntar, remitir adjunto
enclosure carta f adjunta,
documento m adjunto
end (n) fin m, final m
end (v) terminar, finalizar
end of season sale rebajas fpl de fin
de temporada
end product producto m final
end user usuario m final
endorse a cheque/check endosar
un cheque
endorsement (action) endoso m; (on
insurance) suplemento m de póliza
energy-saving (adj)
que ahorra energía
engaged (telephone) (línea) ocupada
engaged tone señal f de comunicar
enter entrar en; (write in) inscribir
enter into (discussion) entablar
enterprise empresa f
entitle autorizar
entitlement derecho m
entrepreneur empresario(-a)
entrepreneurial empresarial
entry (going in) acceso m,
ingreso m, entrada f; (writing)
asiento m, anotación f, registro m
entry visa visado m de entrada
equip equipar
equipment equipo m
equities títulos mpl,
acciones fpl ordinarias
equity capital capital m en acciones

error error m, equivocación f
**errors and omissions excepted (e. &
o.e.)** salvo error u omisión
escape clause cláusula f de excepción
establish establecer, consolidar
establishment (business)
establecimiento m
estimate (n) (calculation)
estimación f, cálculo m,
valoración f; (quote)
presupuesto m
estimate (v) estimar, calcular, valorar
estimated sales ventas fpl estimadas
European Union Unión Europea (UE)
evaluate costs evaluar los costes
evaluation evaluación f, valoración f
exact exacto(-a)
examination (inspection) examen m,
registro m, inspección f; (test)
examen m
examine examinar, revisar, registrar
exceed exceder, sobrepasar, superar
excellent excelente
excess excedente m, exceso m
excess capacity
exceso m de capacidad
excessive excesivo(-a)
exchange (currency) (n) cambio m;
(v) cambiar divisas
exchange (v) (one thing for another)
canjear, intercambiar
exchange rate
tipo m/tasa f de cambio
excise duty impuesto m sobre
el consumo
excluding excepto
exclusion clause cláusula f
de exclusión
exclusive agreement contrato m
en exclusiva
exclusive of tax impuesto m
no incluido
exclusivity exclusividad f, exclusiva f
executive ejecutivo(-a)
exempt exento(-a), dispensado(-a)
exempt (v) eximir, dispensar
exempt from tax exento(-a)
de impuestos
exemption from tax exención fiscal
exercise an option ejercer derecho
de opción
exercise of an option ejercicio m del
derecho de opción

exhibit (v) exponer
exhibition exhibición f, exposición f
exhibitor expositor(a)
expand ampliar, expandir, crecer
expenditure
  gasto m, desembolso m
expense gasto m
expense account cuenta f de gastos
  de representación
expensive caro(-a), costoso(-a)
experienced experimentado(-a)
expert experto(-a)
expire caducar, expirar, vencer
expiry caducidad f,
  expiración f, vencimiento m
expiry date
  fecha f de caducidad/ vencimiento
export (n) exportación f, mercancía f
  exportada; (v) exportar
export department
  departamento de exportación
export licence/permit licencia f/
  permiso m de exportación
export manager
  director(a) de exportación
exporter exportador(a)
exports exportaciones fpl
exposure exposición f
express (adj) rápido(-a), urgente
express delivery entrega f urgente
extend (make longer) extender,
  prolongar, prorrogar
extended credit crédito m a
  largo plazo
extension (longer) ampliación f,
  prolongación f, prórroga f
extension (telephone) extensión f
external audit auditoría f externa
external auditor auditor m externo
external trade comercio m exterior
extra charges/extras gastos mpl
  adicionales, extras mpl

F

face value valor m nominal
facilities
  instalaciones fpl, medios mpl
facility (credit) facilidad f
factor (n) (influence) factor m,
  elemento m, coeficiente m
factor (n) (agent) agente m/f,
  comisionista m/f

factoring charges coste m de la
  gestión de deudas
factory fábrica f
factory price precio de fábrica
fail (go bust) quebrar; (not to
  succeed) fallar, fracasar
failing that en su defecto
failure fracaso m
fair (adj) justo(-a), equitativo(-a)
fair price precio m justo
fair wear and tear
  desgaste m natural
fake (n) falsificación f, imitación f
fall behind
  quedarse atrás, retrasarse
fall due vencer
fall through venirse abajo
false pretences
  medios mpl fraudulentos
fare billete m, pasaje m
farm out work mandar trabajo fuera
fast-selling items artículos mpl de
  fácil venta
faulty imperfecto(-a), defectuoso(-a)
fax (n) telefax m, fax m
fax (v) enviar por fax
feasibility report informe m de
  viabilidad (de un proyecto)
fee (admission) cuota f,
  derechos mpl; (for services)
  honorarios mpl, emolumentos mpl
field sales manager jefe(-a) de
  equipo de ventas
figure cifra f, cantidad f
figures cifras fpl, resultados mpl
file (n) (computer) archivo m; ficha f
  de ordenador; (documents)
  fichero m, expediente m
file (v) **documents**
  archivar documentos
filing cabinet
  archivador m, clasificador m
filing card ficha f (de registro)
fill a gap llenar, ocupar un
  vacío, rellenar
fill a post cubrir un puesto
final demand último
  requerimiento m de pago
final dividend dividendo m final
finalize finalizar, aprobar con
  carácter definitivo
finance (n) finanzas fpl
finance (v) financiar

finance director director(a) de finanzas

finances finanzas fpl

financial financiero(-a)

financial risk riesgo m financiero

financial year ejercicio m económico, año m fiscal

financing financiación f, financiamiento m

fine (n) multa f; (v) multar

fine tuning ajuste fino

finish acabar, terminar

fire damage daños mpl causados por incendio

fire insurance seguro m contra incendios

firm (n) empresa f, firma f, casa f comercial

firm price precio m en firme

first in first out (FIFO) primeras entradas, primeras salidas

first option primera opción f

first-class de primera clase

fiscal measures medidas fpl fiscales

fix (mend) arreglar; (set) fijar

fixed costs costes mpl fijos

fixed exchange rate cambio m fijo

fixed income renta f fija

fixed scale of charges lista f de precios fija

fixed-price agreement acuerdo m/ contrato m a tanto alzado

flat rate tanto m alzado, porcentaje m fijo

flexibility flexibilidad f

flexible flexible

flight information información f de vuelos

flight of capital evasión f/fuga f de capital(es)

flip chart tablero m de hojas sueltas

float (n) (money) fondo m de caja

float a company fundar una compañía

floor (level) piso m

floor plan planta f

floor space superficie f útil

flop (n) fracaso m; (v) fracasar

flotation lanzamiento m de una nueva compañía

flourishing floreciente, próspero(-a)

flow chart/diagram organigrama m/ diagrama m de flujo

fluctuate fluctuar, oscilar

fluctuation fluctuación f, oscilación f

follow up perseguir

follow-up letter carta f de reiteración

for sale en venta

force majeure fuerza f mayor

forced sale venta f forzosa

forecast (n) previsión f, pronóstico m

forecast (v) pronosticar, prever, predecir

foreign extranjero(-a)

foreign currency/exchange divisas fpl, moneda f extranjera

foreign money order giro m postal internacional

forfeit a deposit perder un depósito

forfeiture decomiso m, confiscación f

forge falsificar

forgery (action) falsificación f

form (n) impreso m, formulario m

form of words fórmulas fpl judiciales

formal formal, oficial

forward (v) expedir, enviar

forward buying compra f de futuros

forward market mercado m a futuros

forward rate tipo m de cambio para operaciones a plazo

forwarding address dirección f de reenvío/de reexpedición

forwarding agent expedidor(a)

forwarding instructions instrucciones fpl de envío

franchise (n) franquicia f, concesión f

franchise (v) franquiciar

franchisee concesionario(-a)

franchiser franquiciador(a)

franchising franquicia f, concesión f

franking machine máquina f franqueadora

fraud fraude m, defraudación f, estafa f

free (adj) libre; (no payment) gratuito(-a), gratis, franco

free (adv) (no payment) gratuitamente, gratis

free delivery entrega gratuita

free market mercado m libre

free of tax libre de impuestos

free on board (f.o.b.) franco a bordo

free sample muestra f gratuita

free trade zone zona f franca

freeze (v) *(prices)* congelar
freight *(carriage)* flete m, transporte m, porte m
freight costs gastos mpl de transporte
freight forward porte m debido
freight plane avión m de carga
frequent frecuente, corriente
frozen account cuenta f bloqueada
frozen assets activo m congelado
fulfil/fulfill an order despachar un pedido
full lleno(-a)
full price precio m sin descuento
full refund reembolso m total
full-time a tiempo completo, a jornada completa
fund (n) fondo m
fund (v) asignar fondos, financiar
further to además de, con relación a
future delivery entrega f futura

G

gain (n) *(getting bigger)* aumento m; *(in value)* ganancia f, beneficio m
gain (v) ganar
gap in the market hueco m en el mercado
gearing apalancamiento m
general general
general manager director(a) gerente
general post offfice oficina f central de correos
general strike huelga f general
get into debt endeudarse
get rid of sth. deshacerse de algo
get the sack ser despedido
gift regalo m, obsequio m
gift voucher vale m para un regalo
give *(as gift)* regalar
glut (n) abundancia f
go into business emprender un negocio
going rate precio m vigente
gold card tarjeta f oro
good buy buena compra
good quality buena calidad
good value *(for money)* buen precio
goods mercancías fpl
goodwill fondo m de comercio
government bonds títulos mpl del Estado

government contractor contratista m/f del Estado
graduate trainee licenciado(-a) en prácticas
graduated tax impuesto m progresivo
gram/gramme gramo m
grand total suma f total
gratis gratis, sin pagar
gross (n) *(144)* gruesa f
gross (v) obtener beneficios brutos
gross domestic product (GDP) Producto Interior Bruto (PIB)
gross national product (GNP) Producto Nacional Bruto (PNB)
gross profit beneficio m bruto
gross salary sueldo m bruto
gross weight peso m bruto
group grupo m
grow crecer
growth crecimiento m, desarrollo m
growth rate tasa f de crecimiento
guarantee (n) garantía f, aval m
guarantee (v) avalar, garantizar
guide *(for tourists)* guía m/f
guideline directriz f

H

half (adj) medio(-a)
half (n) mitad f
half-price sale rebajas a mitad de precio
half-year semestre m
hand luggage equipaje m de mano
hand over entregar
handle (v) *(deal with)* ocuparse; *(sell)* comerciar
handling charge gasto m de tramitación
handwritten escrito(-a) a mano
happen ocurrir
harbour/harbor puerto m
hard currency divisas fpl fuertes, moneda f convertible
hard disk disco m duro
haulage company empresa f de transportes
haulage costs/rates coste m/ acarreo m del transporte
head of department jefe(-a) de departamento
head office oficina f central

headquarters (HQ) sede f
heavy costs grandes costes mpl
heavy equipment equipo m pesado
heavy expenditure gran gasto m
heavy goods vehicle (HGV)
  camión m de carga pesada
hectare hectárea f
hidden asset bien m encubierto
hidden reserves reservas fpl ocultas
high interest interés m elevado
high rent alquiler m elevado
high-quality de calidad superior
highly-paid muy bien pagado
highly-priced muy caro(-a)
hire a car alquilar un coche
hire out arrendar
hire purchase (HP) compra f a plazos
hire staff contratar personal
historical figures cifras fpl históricas
hold (n) (ship) bodega f
hold (v) (contain) contener, caber
hold a discussion
  tener una discusión
hold a meeting celebrar una reunión
hold over aplazar, posponer
hold up (v) (delay) retrasar
hold-up (n) (delay) retraso m
holding company sociedad f de
  cartera, 'holding'
home address domicilio m particular
home sales ventas nacionales/en el
  mercado interior
honour/honor a bill pagar una factura
hotel bill factura f de hotel
hour hora f
hourly rate tarifa f horaria
hourly wage salario/sueldo por hora
hourly-paid workers
  trabajadores mpl pagados
  por horas
house (company) casa f comercial
house-to-house selling venta f
  a domicilio
hurry up darse prisa
hypermarket hipermercado m

I

illegal ilegal
illegally ilegalmente
immediate inmediato(-a)
immediately inmediatamente
imperfect imperfecto(-a)

implement (n)
  herramienta f, instrumento m
implement (v) poner en práctica
implementation
  ejecución f, realización f
import (n) importación f
import (v) importar
import duty
  derechos mpl de importación
import licence/permit licencia f
  de importación
import quota cuota f/cupo m
  de importación
importance importancia f
importer importador(a)
imports importaciones fpl
impulse buyer
  comprador(a) impulsivo(-a)
in-house interno(-a), de la casa
incentive incentivo m, estímulo m
incidental expenses gastos mpl
  menores, imprevistos mpl
include incluir
inclusive inclusive
inclusive charge
  precio m todo incluido
inclusive of tax
  impuestos mpl incluidos
income ingresos mpl, renta f
income tax
  impuesto m sobre la renta
incoming call llamada f de fuera
incorporate (a company) constituir
  en sociedad
incorrect incorrecto(-a), erróneo(-a)
incorrectly
  incorrectamente, erróneamente
increase (n) aumento m,
  incremento m; (v) aumentar, subir,
  incrementar
increase (v) in price subir de precio,
  aumentar de precio
incur (costs) incurrir en
incur debts contraer deudas
indebted endeudado(-a)
indemnification indemnización f
indemnify so. for a loss indemnizar a
  alguien por una pérdida
indemnity indemnidad f,
  indemnización f
index (n) (of prices)
  índice m, relación f
index (v) catalogar, clasificar

index-linked ajustado(-a) al coste de la vida
indicator indicador *m*
indirect taxation
imposición *f* indirecta
induction course
curso *m* de iniciación
industrial accident
accidente *m* laboral
industrial design diseño *m* industrial
industrial relations
relaciones *fpl* laborales
industrial tribunal magistratura *f* del trabajo
industrialist industrial *m/f*
industry industria *f*
inefficiency
ineficacia *f*, incompetencia *f*
inefficient ineficaz, incompetente
inflation inflación *f*
inflationary
inflacionario(-a), inflacionista
influence (n) influencia *f*
influence (v) influir
inform informar
information información *f*
infrastructure infraestructura *f*
infringe a patent violar una patente
infringement of patent violación *f* de patente
initial (v)
poner las iniciales a, rubricar
initial capital capital *m* inicial
initiate discussions
iniciar conversaciones
initiative iniciativa *f*
input information introducir datos
inquire preguntar, pedir información
inquiry petición *f* de informes, investigación *f*
insolvent insolvente
inspect
inspeccionar, revisar, examinar
inspection inspección *f*, examen *m*
instalment plazo *m*
instant credit crédito *m* instantáneo
institution institución *f*
institutional investors
inversores *mpl* institucionales
instructions for use modo *m* de empleo, instrucciones *fpl*
instrument *(document)* efecto *m*, documento *m* escrito

insurance seguro *m*
insurance broker
corredor *m* de seguros
insurance premium
prima *f* de seguros
insure asegurar
insurer asegurador(a)
intangible assets activo *m* intangible
interest (n) *(paid on investment)* interés *m*, rédito *m*
interest (v) interesar
interest charges cargos *mpl* en concepto de interés
interest rate tipo *m*, tasa *f* de interés
interface (n) interfaz *m*, conexión *f*
interim payment pago *m* a cuenta
intermediary intermediario(-a)
internal interno(-a)
international trade
comercio *m* internacional
interpret interpretar
interpreter intérprete *m/f*
interrupt interrumpir
intervention price precio *m* de intervención
interview (n) *(for a job)* entrevista *f*
interview (v) *(for a job)* entrevistar
introduce presentar, introducir
introductory offer
oferta *f* de lanzamiento
invalid inválido(-a), nulo(-a)
invalidate invalidar, anular
inventory (n) *(stock)* existencias *fpl*; *(list of contents)* inventario *m*
inventory control control *m* de existencias
invest invertir
investment inversión *f*
investment income renta *f* de inversiones
investor inversor(a)
invisible earnings
ingresos *mpl* invisibles
invisible trade comercio *m* invisible
invite invitar
invoice (n) factura *f*; (v) facturar
invoice number número *m* de factura
invoice value precio *m* facturado
IOU pagaré *m*
irrecoverable debt
deuda *f* incobrable
irredeemable bond
obligación *f* perpetua

irregularities irregularidades *fpl*
irrevocable letter of credit carta *f* de crédito irrevocable
issue a letter of credit abrir una carta de crédito
issue instructions dar instrucciones
item *(on agenda)* punto *m*; *(thing for sale)* artículo *m*
itemized account cuenta *f* detallada
itemized invoice factura *f* detallada

J

job *(employment)* puesto *m* de trabajo, empleo *m*; *(piece of work)* trabajo *m*, tarea *f*
job description descripción *f* del puesto de trabajo
job security seguridad *f* en el empleo
job title cargo *m*
join juntar, ingresar en
joint conjunto(-a)
joint account cuenta *f* conjunta, cuenta en participación
joint managing director codirector(a) gerente
joint signatory signatario *m* colectivo
joint venture empresa *f* conjunta
journal *(accounts)* libro *m* diario
judgment debtor deudor(a) judicial
jump the queue/line saltarse la cola
junior clerk pasante *m/f*, auxiliar *m/f* administrativo(-a)
junk bonds bonos-basura *mpl*
jurisdiction jurisdicción *f*
justify justificar

K

keen competition fuerte competencia
keen prices precios *mpl* competitivos
keep a promise cumplir una promesa
keep up with the demand satisfacer la demanda
key *(on keyboard)* tecla *f*
key industry industria *f* clave
keyboard *(v)* teclear, pasar a máquina
keyboarder operador(a) de teclado
kilo/kilogram kilo *m*, kilogramo *m*

knock down *(v)* *(price)* rematar, rebajar
knock off *(reduce price)* descontar; *(stop work)* terminar de trabajar

L

label *(n)* etiqueta *f*; *(v)* etiquetar
labour/labor costs costes *mpl* laborales
labour/labor disputes conflictos *mpl* laborales
lack of funds falta *f* de fondos
land *(n)* tierra *f*
land *(v)* *(of plane)* aterrizar
land goods at a port descargar mercancías en un puerto
landed costs coste *m* descargado
landing charges gastos *mpl* de descarga
landlord propietario(-a)
lapse *(v)* caducar, prescribir
last quarter último trimestre
late *(adv)* tarde, con retraso
latest último(-a)
launch/launching lanzamiento *m*
law derecho *m*, ley *f*
law courts tribunales *mpl* de justicia
lawful trade comercio *m* legal
lawsuit pleito *m*, juicio *m*, proceso *m*
lawyer abogado(-a)
lay off workers despedir por falta de trabajo
leaflet folleto *m* publicitario
lease *(n)* arrendamiento *m*, arriendo *m*
lease *(v)* *(of landlord)* arrendar, ceder en arriendo; *(of tenant)* arrendar, tomar en arriendo
lease equipment arrendar equipo
lease-back cesión-arrendamiento *f*
leasing arrendamiento *m* financiero, 'leasing' *m*
ledger libro *m* mayor
left *(not right)* izquierdo(-a)
left luggage office consigna *f*
legal *(referring to law)* jurídico(-a), judicial
legal advice asesoramiento *m* jurídico
legal costs/charges costas *fpl* judiciales
legal proceedings proceso *m* judicial

legal status condición *f*/
personalidad *f* jurídica
lend prestar
lender prestamista *m/f*
lending limit límite *m* de crédito
lessee arrendatario(-a), inquilino(-a)
lessor arrendador(a)
let an office alquilar una oficina
letter carta *f*
letter of complaint carta *f*
de reclamación
letter of credit (L/C) carta *f* de crédito
letter of reference
carta *f* de recomendación
level nivel *m*
level off/out nivelarse, estabilizarse
leverage
apalancamiento *m* financiero
levy (n) recaudación *f* de impuestos
levy (v) recaudar, gravar
liabilities pasivo *m*, obligaciones *fpl*
liable for responsable de
liable to sujeto(-a) a
licence licencia *f*, permiso *m*
license
conceder una licencia, autorizar
lien gravamen *m*, derecho *m*
de retención
life assurance seguro *m* de vida
lift an embargo levantar un embargo
limit (n) límite *m*, acotación *f*
limit (v) limitar
limited (liability) company (Ltd)
sociedad *f* de responsabilidad
limitada (S.R.L.)
limited liability
responsabilidad *f* limitada
liquid assets activo *m* líquido
liquidate liquidar
liquidation liquidación *f*
liquidator síndico *m*
liquidity liquidez *f*
list (n) *(catalogue/catalog)* catálogo *m*
list price precio *m* de catálogo
litre/liter litro *m*
load (v) *(computer program)*
cargar (informática)
load a truck cargar un camión
loan (n) préstamo *m*
loan (v) prestar
loan capital empréstito *m*
local call llamada *f* local
lock (n) cerradura *f*

lock (v) cerrar con llave
lock up a shop cerrar una tienda
lock up capital inmovilizar capital
logo logotipo *m*
long credit crédito *m* a largo plazo
long-dated bill letra *f* a largo plazo
long-haul flight
vuelo *m* de larga distancia
long-standing agreement acuerdo de
muchos años
long-term a largo plazo
long-term planning planificación *f* a
largo plazo
loose suelto(-a), a granel
lose an order perder un pedido
lose money perder dinero
loss *(insurance)* siniestro *m*
loss pérdida *f*
loss-leader artículo *m* de reclamo
low sales ventas *fpl* bajas
lower (v) **prices** reducir los precios
luggage equipaje *m*, maletas *fpl*
lump sum pago *m* único,
suma *f* global

M

machinery maquinaria *f*
magazine revista *f*
magazine insert encarte *m*
publicitario de una revista
mail (n) correo *m*, correspondencia *f*
mail (v) mandar por correo, echar
al correo
mail shot publicidad *f* por correo
mail-order pedido *m* por correo
mail-order catalogue/catalog
catálogo *m* de ventas por correo
mailing list lista *f* de destinatarios
mailing shot envío *m* de publicidad
por correo
main building edificio *m* principal
main office oficina *f* principal
maintain *(keep going)*
mantener, sostener
maintenance *(in working order)*
mantenimiento *m*, conservación *f*
major shareholder/stockholder
accionista *m/f* importante
majority mayoría *f*
majority shareholder/stockholder
accionista *m/f* mayoritario

make good

make good *(a defect, loss)* resarcir, compensar
make money ganar dinero
make out *(invoice)* confeccionar, extender
make up for compensar
man (v) asignar personal
man-hour hora-hombre *f*
manage property administrar una propiedad
manage to arreglárselas, conseguir
management *(action)* dirección *f*, gerencia *f*; *(managers)* junta *f* de directores
management course curso *m* de gestión empresarial
management team equipo *m* directivo
management trainee ejecutivo(-a) en formación
manager *(of branch, shop)* gerente *m/f*, encargado(-a)
managerial staff personal *m* administrativo
managing director (MD) director(a) gerente
manifest manifiesto *m*
manning levels niveles *mpl* de dotación de personal
manpower mano *f* de obra
manual manual
manual work trabajo *m* manual
manual worker obrero(-a)
manufacture (v) fabricar, manufacturar
manufactured goods productos *mpl* manufacturados
manufacturer fabricante *m*
manufacturing costs costes *mpl* de fabricación
manufacturing overheads gastos *mpl* generales de fabricación
margin *(profit)* margen *m*
marginal pricing fijación *f* de precios marginal
marine insurance seguro marítimo
maritime trade comercio *m* marítimo
mark (n) marca *f*, señal *f*; *(German currency)* marco *m*
mark (v) marcar, señalar, indicar
mark down rebajar
mark up aumentar, recargar

mark-up *(profit margin)* margen *m* de beneficio
market (n) *(sales)* mercado *m*
market (v) vender
market analysis análisis *m* de mercado
market forces fuerzas *fpl* del mercado
market leader líder *m* del mercado
market opportunities oportunidades *fpl* de mercado
market penetration penetración *f* en el mercado
market research estudio *m*/ investigación *f* de mercado
market share cuota *f* de mercado
market trends tendencias *fpl* del mercado
marketing comercialización *f*, mercadotecnia *f*, 'marketing' *m*
marketing department departamento *m* de 'marketing'
marketing manager director(a) de 'marketing'
marketing strategy estrategia *f* de 'marketing'
mass market product producto destinado a un mercado de masas
mass media medios *mpl* de comunicación
mass production producción *f* en serie/a gran escala
material material *m*
maternity leave licencia *f* por maternidad
matter (n) *(for discussion)* cuestión *f*, asunto *m*
matter (v) importar
maturity date fecha *f* de vencimiento
maximum (adj) máximo(-a)
maximum (n) máximo *m*
mean (n) promedio *m*, media *f*
mean annual increase aumento *m* anual medio
means recursos *mpl*, medios *mpl*
measurement of profitability evaluación *f*/medición *f* de la rentabilidad
medium mediano(-a)
medium-term plazo *m* medio
meet *(be satisfactory)* cumplir, satisfacer; *(so.)* encontrarse (con), reunirse

meet a deadline
cumplir un plazo establecido
meet a demand satisfacer/atender
una demanda
meet a target cumplir un objetivo,
alcanzar una meta
meeting reunión f, junta f, asamblea f
memo memorándum m, nota f
mention mencionar
merchandise (n)
mercancías fpl, género m
merchandize a product comercializar
un producto
merchandizing
comercialización f, mercadeo m
merchant negociante m/f,
comerciante m/f, mercader m
merchant bank banco m de
negocios, banco mercantil
merge fusionar
merger fusión f
message mensaje m, recado m
middle management
mandos mpl intermedios
middle-sized company
empresa mediana
middleman intermediario(-a)
million millón m
minimum (adj) mínimo(-a)
minimum (n) mínimo m
minimum payment pago m mínimo
minimum wage salario m mínimo
minority minoría f
minority shareholder/stockholder
accionista m minoritario
minus factor factor m negativo
minute (n) (time) minuto m
minute (v) anotar, tomar nota
minutes (n) (of meeting) acta f de
la reunión
miscalculate calcular mal
miscalculation error m de cálculo
miscellaneous misceláneo(-a)
miss (not to hit) errar
miss (not to meet) no encontrar;
(train, plane) perder
mistake equivocación f, error m
misunderstanding malentendido m
mixed economy economía f mixta
mobile phone teléfono m móvil
mobilize capital movilizar capital
mock-up maqueta f, modelo m
a escala

mode of payment modo m de pago
model (n) (small copy) maqueta f,
modelo m a escala; (style of
product) modelo m
model agreement prototipo m
de contrato
modem modem m
moderate (adj) moderado(-a)
monetary monetario(-a)
money dinero m
money order giro m postal
money supply oferta f monetaria
money up front
pago m por adelantado
monitor (n) (screen) pantalla f
monitor (v) controlar, comprobar
monopoly monopolio m
month mes m
month-end accounts cuentas fpl de
fin de mes
monthly (adj) mensual
monthly payments
pagos mpl mensuales
monthly statement estado m de
cuenta mensual
mortgage (n) hipoteca f
mortgage (v) hipotecar
motivated motivado(-a)
motivation motivación f
multilateral agreement
acuerdo m multilateral
multinational (n) multinacional f
multiple (adj) múltiple
multiple entry visa visado m de
entradas múltiples
multiple store
cadena f de grandes almacenes
multiplication multiplicación f
multiply multiplicar

N

nationalized industry
industria f nacionalizada
nationwide de ámbito nacional
natural resources
recursos mpl naturales
natural wastage pérdida f de
trabajadores por jubilación
negotiable negociable
negotiable instrument
instrumento m negociable
negotiate negociar, gestionar

negotiation negociación f
negotiator negociador(-a)
net (adj) neto(-a)
net assets/worth activo m neto
net income/salary salario m/ sueldo m neto
net margin margen m neto
net price precio m neto
net profit beneficio m neto
net sales ventas fpl netas
net weight peso m neto
net yield rendimiento m neto
network (v) (computers) difundir a través de la red de emisoras
niche hueco m de un mercado
nil nada f, cero m
nil return declaración f de ingresos nulos
no-claims bonus prima f por ausencia de siniestralidad
nominal capital capital m nominal
nominal value valor m nominal
nominee apoderado(-a)
non profit-making sin fines lucrativos
non-negotiable instrument documento m no negociable
non-payment (of a debt) impago m
non-refundable deposit depósito m no reembolsable
non-returnable packing envase m no retornable
notary public notario m
note (n) nota f
note (v) anotar
notice (time allowed) plazo m
notification notificación f
notify notificar, avisar
null nulo(-a)
number (n) (figure) número m
number (v) numerar
numeric keypad teclado m numérico

O

obey obedecer
objective (adj) objetivo(-a)
objective (n) objetivo m
obligation (duty) obligación f, compromiso m
obsolescence caducidad f, obsolescencia f
obsolete obsoleto(-a), anticuado(-a)

obtain obtener, conseguir
obtainable asequible
occur ocurrir
off (away from work) ausente del trabajo; (cancelled) cancelado(-a), suspendido(-a)
off-peak fuera de horas punta
off-season temporada f baja
offer (n) oferta f
offer (v) (to buy) ofrecer
office oficina f, despacho m
office hours horario m de oficina
office staff personal m administrativo
offices to let oficinas fpl de alquiler
official (adj) oficial
official (n) funcionario(-a)
offshore en aguas territoriales
oil (petroleum) petróleo m
oil price precio m del crudo/ del petróleo
old viejo(-a), antiguo(-a)
on a short-term basis a corto plazo
on account a cuenta
on approval a prueba
on behalf of en nombre de
on business por asuntos de negocios
on condition that a condición de que
on credit a crédito
on order pedido(-a)
on sale a la venta
on time a tiempo
one-off único(-a)
open (adj) (not closed) abierto(-a)
open (v) (start new business) abrir/emprender un negocio
open a bank account abrir una cuenta bancaria
open a line of credit abrir una línea de crédito
open a meeting abrir la sesión
open account cuenta f abierta
open credit crédito m abierto
open market mercado m libre
open ticket billete m abierto
open-plan office oficina f de distribución modificable
opening balance saldo m inicial
opening hours horario m comercial
opening stock existencias fpl iniciales
opening time hora f de apertura

operate obrar, dirigir, hacer funcionar
operating costs/expenses gastos *mpl* de explotación
operating manual manual *m* de funcionamiento
operating profit beneficio *m* de explotación
operation operación *f*
operational costs gastos *mpl* de explotación
operator operario(-a), maquinista *m/f*
opinion poll encuesta *f*, sondeo *m* de opinión
option to purchase opción *f* de compra
optional extras extras *mpl* opcionales
order (n) *(for goods)* pedido *m*; *(instruction)* orden *f*; *(money)* libramiento *m*, orden *f* de pago
order (v) *(goods)* hacer un pedido, encargar
order fulfilment despacho *m* de pedidos
order number número *m* de pedido
order processing preparación *f* de pedidos
order, on pedido(-a)
ordinary shares/stocks acciones *fpl* ordinarias
organization chart organigrama *m*
organize organizar
origin origen *m*
original (adj) original
out of date anticuado(-a), caducado(-a)
out of stock agotado(-a)
out of work sin empleo, sin trabajo
outgoings desembolsos *mpl*
outlay desembolso *m*, gasto *m*
output (n) *(goods)* producción *f*, rendimiento *m*
outside line línea *f* exterior
outsize (OS) talla *f* muy grande
outstanding *(exceptional)* notable, destacado(-a), sobresaliente; *(unpaid)* pendiente
outstanding debts deudas *fpl* pendientes
outstanding orders pedidos *mpl* pendientes
overbook reservar con exceso

overbooking sobrecontratación *m*, 'overbooking' *m*
overcapacity sobrecapacidad *f*
overcharge (n) precio *m* excesivo, regargo *m*
overcharge (v) cargar en exceso, cobrar de más
overdraft sobregiro *m*, descubierto *m*
overdrawn account cuenta *f* en descubierto
overdue vencido(-a), atrasado(-a)
overhead costs/overheads gastos *mpl* generales, gastos de producción
overproduction sobreproducción *f*
overseas trade comercio *m* exterior
overspend gastar excesivamente
overstocks exceso *m* de existencias
overtime horas *fpl* extraordinarias
overtime pay tarifa *f* de horas extras
owe deber
owing to debido a, a causa de
own label goods productos *mpl* de marca propia
owner amo *m*, propietario(-a)
ownership propiedad *f*

P

pack (n) paquete *m*
pack (v) embalar, envasar, empaquetar
package deal transacción *f* global
packaging material material *m* de embalaje
packer embalador(a), empaquetador(a)
packing *(material)* embalaje *m*
packing list/slip lista *f* de contenidos
pact pacto *m*
paid *(invoice)* pagado(-a)
pallet bandeja *f*, paleta *f*
paper loss pérdida *f* sobre el papel
paper profit beneficio *m* sobre el papel
paperwork papeleo *m*
par value valor *m* a la par
parcel (n) paquete *m*
parcel post servicio *m* de paquetes postales
parent company sociedad *f* matriz
part exchange canje *m* parcial

part-time employment empleo *m* a tiempo parcial
part-time work trabajo *m* por horas
partial payment pago *m* parcial
particulars detalles *mpl*, pormenores *mpl*
partner socio(-a), asociado(-a)
party parte *f*
patent applied for patente *f* solicitada
patent pending patente en tramitación
pay (n) *(salary)* paga *f*
pay a bill pagar una cuenta
pay an invoice pagar una factura
pay back devolver
pay by credit card pagar con tarjeta de crédito
pay cash pagar al contado, en efectivo
pay cheque/check cheque *m* de sueldo/de salario
pay in advance pagar por adelantado
pay out pagar, desembolsar, abonar
pay phone teléfono *m* público
pay rise aumento *m* de sueldo
payable in advance pagadero por adelantado
payable on delivery pagadero a la entrega
payable on demand pagadero a la vista
payee portador(a), beneficiario(-a)
payer pagador(a)
payment pago *m*, remuneración *f*
payment by cheque/check pago *m* mediante cheque
payment in cash pago *m* en metálico, pago en efectivo
payment on account pago *m* a cuenta
peak period horas *fpl* punta
peg prices estabilizar los precios
penalize penalizar, sancionar
penalty clause cláusula *f* penal
pending pendiente
penetrate a market penetrar un mercado
pension pensión *f*
per hour/day/week/annum por hora, al día, por semana, al año
percentage porcentaje *m*, tanto *m* por ciento

percentage discount porcentaje *m* de descuento
period periodo *m*, plazo *m*
peripherals periféricos *mpl*
perishable goods mercancías *fpl* perecederas
permission permiso *m*
permit (n) permiso *m*, licencia *f*
permit (v) permitir
personal allowances deducciones *fpl* personales
personal assistant (PA) ayudante *m/f*, secretario(-a) personal
personal computer (PC) ordenador *m* personal
personnel personal *m*
personnel manager director(a)/ jefe(-a) de personal
peseta *(currency)* peseta *f*
peso *(currency)* peso *m*
petty cash caja *f* para gastos menores
petty expenses gastos *mpl* menores
phase in introducir gradualmente
phase out reducir/retirar gradualmente
phone (n) teléfono *m*
phone (v) telefonear, llamar (por teléfono)
phone call llamada *f* telefónica
phone card tarjeta *f* telefónica
photocopier fotocopiadora *f*
photocopy (n) fotocopia *f*
photocopy (v) fotocopiar
pie chart gráfico *m* circular, gráfico sectorial
piece rate precio *m* a destajo
piecework trabajo *m* a destajo
pilot scheme programa *m* piloto
place sitio *m*, lugar *m*
place an order cursar un pedido
place of work lugar *m* de trabajo
plan (n) *(drawing)* plano *m*; *(project)* plan *m*, proyecto *m*
plan (v) planear, planificar
plane avión *m*
plant (n) *(machinery)* maquinaria *f*
plug (n) *(electric)* enchufe *m*
plug (v) *(publicize)* dar publicidad
plus factor factor *m* positivo
point of sale (p.o.s., POS) punto *m* de venta

point out apuntar, indicar, señalar
policy política f
poor quality mala calidad f
poor service servicio m deficiente
popular prices precios mpl populares
port (computer) conexión f;
(harbour/harbor) puerto m
port of call puerto m de escala
port of embarkation puerto m
de embarque
portable portátil
portfolio cartera f (de valores)
POS material (point of sale material)
publicidad f en el punto de venta
position (job)
puesto m, cargo m, plaza f
positive positivo(-a)
possess poseer
post (n) (job)
puesto m; (letters) correo m
post (v) enviar, mandar por correo
post free sin gastos de franqueo
postage franqueo m, tarifa f postal
postage and packing (p & p) (gastos
de) franqueo y embalaje
postage paid franqueo m
concertado, con porte pagado
postal charges
gastos mpl de franqueo
postal rates tarifas fpl postales
postcode código m postal
poste restante lista f de correos
postpaid porte m pagado,
franqueo m concertado
postpone aplazar, posponer
postponement aplazamiento m
potential market
mercado m potencial
pound (money) libra f;
(weight: 0.45kg) libra f
power of attorney
poder m notarial, poderes mpl
premises local m, edificio m
premium (insurance)
prima f de seguros
premium offer
obsequio m publicitario
prepack/prepackage
preempaquetar
prepaid pagado(-a) por adelantado
prepayment pago m por adelantado
present (adj) (being there) presente;
(now) actual

present (n) (gift)
regalo m, obsequio m
present (v) (document) presentar
presentation presentación f
press conference conferencia f
de prensa
press release comunicado m
de prensa
pretax profit beneficio m antes
de deducir los impuestos
prevention prevención f
price (n) precio m
price (v) poner precio a
price ceiling límite m de precios
price controls control m de precios
price ex warehouse precio m puesto
en almacén, franco en almacén
price ex works precio m en fábrica,
franco en fábrica
price label etiqueta f de precio
price list lista f de precios
price tag etiqueta f de precio
price war guerra f de precios
price/earnings ratio (P/E ratio)
relación f precio-ganancias
pricing policy política f de precios
primary industry sector m primario
prime cost coste m de producción
principal (adj) principal
principal (n) (money) principal m;
(person) mandante m
principle principio m
print out imprimir
printer (machine) impresora f
printout impresión f
private enterprise empresa f privada
private property propiedad f privada
private sector sector m privado
privatization privatización f
privatize privatizar
pro forma (invoice) factura f
pro forma
pro rata a prorrata, a prorrateo
probation period periodo m
de prueba
problem area asunto m problemático
problem solver
mediador m de conflictos
process (v) (deal with) preparar,
elaborar, tramitar
processing of information
tratamiento m de la información
product producto m

product advertising

product advertising anuncio *m* del producto
product design diseño *m* de productos
product line gama *f*/línea *f* de productos
product mix gama *f* de productos de una compañía
production *(making)* producción *f*
production department departamento *m* de producción
production target objetivo *m* de producción
productive productivo(-a)
productivity productividad *f*
productivity agreement acuerdo *m* de productividad
professional *(n)* profesional *m/f*
professional qualifications títulos *mpl* profesionales
profit ganancia *f*, beneficio *m*
profit after tax beneficio *m* neto de impuestos
profit and loss account cuenta *f* de pérdidas y ganancias
profit before tax beneficio *m* antes de deducir los impuestos
profit centre/center centro *m* de beneficios
profit margin margen *m* de beneficio
profitability *(making a profit)* rentabilidad *f*
profitable rentable, productivo(-a), lucrativo(-a)
program *(computer)* programar
programme/program programa *m*
progress report informe *m* sobre la marcha de un trabajo
progressive tax impuesto *m* progresivo
project *(plan)* proyecto *m*
project manager director(a) de proyecto
projected sales ventas *fpl* previstas
promissory note pagaré *m*, letra *f* al propio cargo
promote *(advertise)* promocionar
promote *(give better job)* ascender
promotion *(publicity)* promoción *f*; *(to better job)* ascenso *m*
promotional budget presupuesto *m* de promoción

prompt payment pronto pago *m*
prompt service servicio *m* rápido
proportion parte *f*, proporción *f*
proportional proporcional
propose to *(do sth.)* proponer(se)
proprietor propietario *m*, dueño *m*
proprietress propietaria *f*, dueña *f*
prosecution *(legal action)* procesamiento *m*
prospective buyer posible comprador(a)
prospects perspectivas *fpl*
prospectus prospecto *m*, folleto *m*
protest *(v)* protestar
protest strike huelga *f* de protesta
provided that/providing a condición de que
provision *(condition)* disposición *f*, estipulación *f*
provisional budget presupuesto *m* provisional
proviso condición *f*, salvedad *f*
proxy *(person)* poderhabiente *m/f*, apoderado(-a)
proxy vote voto *m* por poderes
public finance finanzas *fpl* públicas
public holiday fiesta *f* oficial, fiesta nacional
Public Limited Company (Plc) sociedad *f* anónima (S.A.)
public relations (PR) relaciones *fpl* públicas
public sector sector *m* público
public transport transporte *m* público
publicity publicidad *f*
publicity budget presupuesto *m* publicitario/de publicidad
publicize dar publicidad, divulgar
purchase *(n)* compra *f*; *(v)* comprar
purchase tax impuesto *m* de venta
purchaser comprador(a)
purchasing compra *f*
purchasing power poder *m* adquisitivo
put back *(later)* aplazar
put in writing poner por escrito
put into practice poner en práctica

Q

qualified *(skilled)* competente, cualificado(-a)

qualify as obtener/sacar el título de
quality control control *m* de calidad
quantity cantidad *f*
quantity discount descuento *m* por cantidad
quarter *(25%)* cuarto *m*, cuarta parte *f*; *(three months)* trimestre *m*
quarterly (adj) trimestral
quay muelle *m*
quorum quórum *m*
quota cupo *m*
quotation/quote (n) *(estimate of cost)* cotización *f*, presupuesto *m*
quote (v) *(estimate costs)* cotizar, calcular, ofrecer un precio

R

rail/railway ferrocarril *m*
railway station estación *f* de ferrocarril
raise (v) *(increase)* aumentar, subir
raise an invoice preparar una factura
raise money conseguir fondos
random check chequeo *m* al azar
random error error *m* aleatorio
random sample muestra *f* aleatoria
range gama *f*
rate (n) *(amount)* tasa *f*, coeficiente *m*, índice *m*; *(price)* precio *m*, tarifa *f*
rate of exchange tipo *m* de cambio
rate of inflation tasa *f* de inflación
rating clasificación *f*
ratio razón *f*, relación *f*
rationalize racionalizar
raw materials materias *fpl* primas
reach a decision tomar una decisión
reach an agreement llegar a un acuerdo
reaction reacción *f*
ready listo(-a), preparado(-a)
ready cash efectivo *m*
real estate bienes *mpl* raíces, propiedad *f* inmobiliaria
real income/wages ingreso *m* real, salarios *mpl* reales
realizable assets activo *m* realizable
realize *(understand)* darse cuenta
realize assets realizar activos
realize property liquidar propiedades
reapply volver a presentarse
reappoint volver a nombrar

reassess revaluar
rebate *(money back)* reembolso *m*
receipt *(paper)* recibo *m*, resguardo *m*; *(receiving)* recepción *f*
receipts ingresos *mpl*, entradas *fpl*
receivables efectos *mpl* a cobrar
receive recibir
receiver *(liquidator)* síndico *m*
reception recepción *f*, acogida *f*
reception desk recepción *f*
receptionist recepcionista *m/f*
recession recesión *f*
recognize a union reconocer a un sindicato
recommend *(say sth. is good)* recomendar; *(suggest action)* aconsejar
reconcile cuadrar, ajustar
reconciliation reconciliación *f*, concertación *f*
record (n) *(better than before)* récord *m*; *(of events)* documento *m*
record (v) registrar, anotar
record sales récord *m* de ventas
records archivos *mpl*
recover *(get better)* recuperarse, mejorar; *(get sth. back)* recuperar, recobrar
recovery *(getting better)* reactivación *f*, mejoría *f*; *(getting sth. back)* recuperación *f*, rescate *m*
recruit new staff reclutar personal
recycle reciclar
recycled paper papel *m* reciclado
red tape burocracia *f*, papeleo *m*
redeem amortizar, redimir
redemption *(of a loan)* amortización *f*, rescate *m*
redemption date fecha *f* de amortización, fecha de rescate
reduce reducir, rebajar, recortar
reduce a price rebajar/reducir un precio
reduced rate precio *m* reducido, tarifa *f* reducida
reduction rebaja *f*, reducción *f*
redundancy desempleo *m*, despido *m*
redundant redundante
refer *(pass to so.)* remitir; *(to item)* referirse, mencionar

reference referencia f
reference number
número m de referencia
refund (n) devolución f, reembolso m
refund (v) reembolsar, devolver
refundable deposit
depósito m reembolsable
refusal negativa f, rechazo m
refuse (v) rehusar, negar(se),
rechazar
regarding relativo a, en cuanto a
regardless of sin tener en cuenta
register (n) (official list) registro m
register (v) (in official list) registrar,
inscribir en un registro;
(letter) certificar
registered letter carta f certificada
registered office domicilio m social
registered trademark
marca f registrada
Registrar of Companies
Registro m Mercantil
registration
registro m, inscripción f, matrícula f
registry registro m
regular (at same time) regular;
(ordinary) normal, ordinario(-a),
corriente
regular customer cliente m/f habitual
regulate (by law) reglamentar
regulations
normas fpl, reglamento m
reinvest reinvertir
reinvestment reinversión f
reject (n) producto m defectuoso
reject (v) rechazar
rejection rechazo m
relating to referente, relativo a
relations relaciones fpl
release (v) (make public)
divulgar, publicar
release dues
despachar pedidos atrasados
reliability fiabilidad f
reliable
fiable, de confianza, cumplidor(a)
rely on depender de
remain (be left) quedar, sobrar
remainder (things left) resto m
remit by cheque/check remitir
por cheque
remittance envío m, giro m
remunerate remunerar

remuneration remuneración f
render an account presentar una
cuenta/una factura
renew a bill of exchange renovar
una letra de cambio
renew a lease
prorrogar un arrendamiento
renewal of a bill renovación de
una letra
renewal of a lease prórroga f de
un arrendamiento
rent (n) alquiler m, renta f,
arrendamiento m
rent (v) (pay money for)
alquilar, arrendar
rental alquiler m
reorder (n) nuevo pedido m
reorder (v) renovar un pedido
reorder level nivel m de existencias
para nuevos pedidos
reorganization reorganización f
reorganize reorganizar
repay pagar, reembolsar, devolver
repayable reembolsable
repeat an order renovar un pedido
repeat order
pedido m suplementario
replacement (item)
reemplazo m, repuesto m
replacement value
valor m de reposición
reply (n) respuesta f, contestación f
reply (v) responder, contestar
report (n) informe m, memoria f
report (v) informar
report to so. rendir cuentas a alguien
represent representar, ser agente de
representative representante m/f
request (n) ruego m,
petición f, solicitud f
request (v) pedir, solicitar
request, on a petición
require requerir, exigir
requirements
necesidades fpl, requisitos mpl
resale reventa f
rescue (n) rescate m
rescue (v) salvar, rescatar
research (n) investigación f
research (v) investigar
research and development (R & D)
investigación y desarrollo (I+D)
researcher investigador(a)

reservation reserva *f*

reserve (n) *(money)* reserva *f*; *(supplies)* reservas *fpl*

reserve *(room, table)* reservar

residence residencia *f*

resident (adj) residente

resign resignar, dimitir

resources recursos *mpl*

response respuesta *f*, reacción *f*

responsibility responsabilidad *f*

responsible *(for)* responsable

responsible to so. ser responsable ante alguien

restock renovar existencias, repostar

restrict restringir, limitar

restrictive practices prácticas *fpl* restrictivas

restructure reestructurar

restructuring of a loan consolidación *f* de un préstamo

result from resultar de, derivar de

result in resultar

results *(company's)* resultados *mpl*

resume negotiations reanudar las negociaciones

retail (v) vender al por menor

retail price precio *m* al por menor

retailer detallista *m/f*, minorista *m/f*

retention retención *f*

retire *(from job)* jubilarse, retirarse

retirement age edad *f* de jubilación

retrain reciclar

retrenchment reducción *f* de gastos

retrieval recuperación *f*

retrieve recuperar

retroactive retroactivo(-a)

return (n) *(going back)* vuelta *f*, regreso *m*; *(sending back)* devolución *f*

return (n) *(interest)* rédito *m*; *(profit)* ganancia *f*, rendimiento *m*; *(declaration)* declaración *f*

return address remite *m*, remitente *m*

return on investment (ROI) rendimiento *m* de la inversión

returns *(unsold goods)* productos *mpl* devueltos sin vender

revalue revaluar

revenue ingreso *m*

reverse (adj) revertido(-a)

reverse charge call llamada *f* a cobro revertido

reverse the charges llamar a cobro revertido

revoke revocar

revolving credit crédito *m* renovable

right (adj) *(not left)* derecho(-a); *(not wrong)* correcto(-a)

right (n) *(legal title)* derecho *m*

right of way derecho *m* de paso

rightful owner propietario(-a) legítimo(-a)

rights issue emisión *f* de derechos

rise (n) *(increase)* alza *f*, subida *f*; *(salary)* aumento *m* de salario

rise (v) subir

risk (n) riesgo *m*

risk (v) *(money)* arriesgar

risk capital capital-riesgo *m*

risky arriesgado(-a)

rival company empresa *f* competidora

road carretera *f*

road transport transporte *m* por carretera

rock-bottom prices precios *mpl* reventados

roll over credit/debt refinanciar un crédito/una deuda

room *(hotel)* habitación *f*; *(space)* espacio *m*

room service servicio *m* de habitaciones de un hotel

rough calculation/estimate cálculo *m* aproximado

round down redondear por defecto

round up redondear por exceso

routine work trabajo *m* rutinario

royalty canon *m*, derechos *mpl* de autor

rule (n) norma *f*, regla *f*, reglamento *m*

rule (v) *(give decision)* decidir, decretar

ruling (n) decisión *f*, fallo *m*

run (v) *(be in force)* ser válido, regir; *(manage)* dirigir, llevar

run into debt endeudarse, adeudarse

run out of stock agotar las existencias

running costs gastos *mpl* corrientes

running total total *m* acumulado

rush hour horas punta/de mayor afluencia

rush order pedido *m* urgente

S

sack so. despedir a alguien
safe (n) caja f fuerte, caja de caudales
safe investment inversión f segura
safeguard proteger
safety seguridad f
safety precautions precauciones fpl, medidas fpl de precaución
safety regulations normas fpl de seguridad
salaried asalariado(-a)
salary salario m, sueldo m
salary review revisión f de sueldos
sale (n) (at a low price) liquidación f, saldo m, rebajas fpl; (selling) venta f
sales ventas fpl
sales budget presupuesto m de ventas
sales campaign campaña f de ventas
sales conference reunión f de ventas
sales department sección f de ventas
sales figures cifras fpl de ventas
sales forecast previsión f de ventas
sales manager director(a) de ventas, director(a) comercial
sales people personal m de ventas
sales target objetivo m de ventas
sales tax impuesto m sobre la venta
salesman (in shop) vendedor(a); (representative) representante m/f
salvage (n) (action) salvamento m, rescate m
salvage (v) salvar
sample (n) (part) muestra f
sampling (testing) muestreo m por áreas
satisfy (customer) satisfacer
saturate the market saturar el mercado
save (v) (money) ahorrar; (not waste) ahorrar; (on computer) archivar, guardar
saving ahorro m
savings account cuenta f de ahorro
scale down/up reducir/aumentar a escala
scheduled flight vuelo m regular
scrip issue emisión f de acciones gratuitas
sealed tenders ofertas fpl lacradas/cerradas

season (time of year) estación f
seasonal demand demanda f estacional
seasonal variations variaciones fpl de temporada/estacionales
second (adj) segundo(-a)
secondary secundario(-a)
secondhand de segunda mano
seconds artículos mpl con desperfectos
secret (adj) secreto(-a)
secretarial college escuela f de secretariado
secretary secretario(-a)
sector sector m
secure funds conseguir fondos
secured creditor acreedor(a) con garantía
secured loan préstamo m garantizado
securities títulos mpl, valores mpl
security guard guardia m de seguridad, vigilante m
security of employment seguridad f de empleo
security of tenure derecho m de ocupación
seize embargar, confiscar, incautar, secuestrar
seizure embargo m, incautación f, secuestro m
self-employed autónomo(-a)
self-financing autofinanciado(-a)
sell vender
sell forward vender a futuros
sell-by date fecha f de caducidad
selling (n) venta f
semi-skilled workers obreros mpl semicualificados
send a package by airmail enviar un paquete por correo aéreo
sender remitente m/f
senior manager/executive gerente m/f, director(a) principal
separate (adj) separado(-a)
serial number número m de serie
serve a customer atender a un cliente
service (n) (dealing with customers) servicio m; (of machine) revisión f
service (v) (a machine) revisar
service centre/center centro m de reparaciones

service charge suplemento m por el servicio

service department servicio m de mantenimiento

service manual manual m de mantenimiento

set (adj) fijo(-a)

set price precio m fijo

set up a company crear/fundar una compañía

setback revés m

settle (an invoice) saldar, pagar

settle an account liquidar una cuenta, saldar una cuenta

settlement (payment) finiquito m, pago m

share (n) (in a company) acción f

share (v) (divide among) dividir, repartir; (use with so.) compartir

share certificate título m/certificado m de una acción

shareholder accionista m/f

shareholding tenencia f de acciones

shelf estantería f, anaquel m

shelf life of a product periodo m de conservación de un producto

shift (n) (team of workers) turno m

shift work trabajo m por turnos

ship (n) barco m, buque m

ship (v) enviar, expedir

shipment envío m, carga f

shipper expedidor(a), transportista m/f

shipping envío m, expedición f

shipping charges/costs costes mpl de envío

shipping instructions instrucciones fpl de envío

shop tienda f

shop around comparar precios

shop assistant dependiente(-a)

shop window escaparate m

shoplifting robo m/hurto m en las tiendas

shopper comprador(a)

shopping centre/mall centro m comercial

short credit crédito m a corto plazo

short of escaso(-a)

short-term (adj) a corto plazo

short-term contract contrato m de corta duración

short-term loan préstamo m a corto plazo

shortage escasez f, falta f

shortlist (n) preselección f, terna f

shortlist (v) preseleccionar

show a profit mostrar un beneficio

sideline negocio m suplementario

sight draft giro m a la vista

sign (n) señal f, letrero m, rótulo m

sign (v) firmar

signatory signatario(-a), firmante m/f

signature firma f

simple interest interés m simple

site sitio m, lugar m, solar m

site engineer ingeniero(-a) de obra

situation (state of affairs) situación f

situations vacant ofertas fpl de trabajo

skeleton staff personal m reducido al mínimo

skill habilidad f, destreza f

skilled labour/labor mano f de obra cualificada

slack flojo(-a), débil

slash (prices, credit terms) reducir drásticamente

sleeping partner socio m comanditario/en comandita

slip (n) (mistake) error m; (piece of paper) resguardo m

slow payer moroso(-a)

slump in sales caída f de las ventas

small businesses pequeñas empresas fpl

small-scale a pequeña escala

social costs costes mpl sociales

social security seguridad f social

socio-economic groups grupos mpl socioeconómicos

soft currency moneda f débil, moneda no convertible

software programa m informático, 'software' m

sole único(-a), exclusivo(-a)

sole agent representante m/f, agente m/f en exclusiva

sole owner propietario(-a) único(-a)

solicit orders solicitar pedidos

solicitor abogado(-a)

solution solución f

solve a problem resolver/solucionar un problema

solvency solvencia f

solvent (adj) solvente
source of income fuente f
de ingresos
spare part
pieza f de recambio, repuesto m
special offer oferta f especial
specification especificación f
specify especificar, precisar, indicar
spend (money) gastar; (time) pasar
spinoff efecto m indirecto
sponsor (n)
patrocinador(a), padrino m
sponsor (v) patrocinar
sponsorship patrocinio m
spot cash pago m al contado,
dinero m en mano
spot price
precio m de entrega inmediata
spot purchase compra f al contado
spread a risk repartir un riesgo
stability estabilidad f
stabilize estabilizar(se)
stable prices precios mpl estables
staff meeting reunión f/asamblea f
de personal
staged payments pagos mpl
por etapas
stagger escalonar
stamp (n) (post) sello m
stamp (v) (letter) poner un sello (en
un sobre), franquear
stamp duty impuesto m del timbre
stand (n) (at exhibition) local m de
exposición, 'stand' m
standard (adj)
normal, estándar, corriente
standard (n) norma f, modelo m
standard rate (of tax) tasa f de
impuestos normal
standardize
normalizar, estandarizar
standby ticket billete m en lista
de espera
standing fama f, reputación f
staple industry industria f principal
start (v) comenzar, empezar
start-up costs costes mpl de puesta
en marcha
starting date fecha f inicial
starting salary salario m inicial
state (n) (condition) estado m
state-of-the-art
muy moderno(-a), al día

statement of account estado m
de cuentas
station (train) estación f
statistical analysis
análisis m estadístico
statistics estadísticas fpl
status status m, posición f
status inquiry petición f de informes
sobre crédito
statute of limitations
ley f de prescripción
statutory holiday/vacation
vacaciones fpl reglamentarias
sterling libra f esterlina
stiff competition competencia f dura
stipulate estipular
stock (adj) (normal) normal;
(in a company) acciones fpl
stock (n) (goods) existencias fpl;
(in a company) acciones fpl
stock (v) (goods) almacenar
stock control
control m de existencias
stock exchange bolsa f
stock list inventario m, lista f
de existencias
stock market mercado m de
valores, bolsa f
stock size talla f, tamaño m corriente
stock up acumular
stockbroker corredor(a)/agente m/f
de bolsa
stockist distribuidor(a)
stocktaking inventario m
stocktaking sale liquidación f
de inventario
stop (v) (doing sth.) dejar,
parar, cesar
stop a cheque/check detener el pago
de un cheque
stop payments suspender pagos
storage (n) (computer)
almacenaje m; (cost) coste m
de almacenaje; (in warehouse)
depósito m, almacenamiento m
storage capacity capacidad f de
almacenamiento/de almacenaje
storage facilities instalaciones fpl de
almacenamiento/de almacenaje
store (n) (place where goods are
kept) almacén m, depósito m
store (v) (in warehouse) almacenar
storeroom almacén m, depósito m

strategic planning
   planificación f estratégica
strategy estrategia f
street directory
   guía f urbana, callejero m
strike (n) huelga f
strike (v) estar en huelga
striker huelguista m/f
strong currency moneda f fuerte
subcontract (n) subcontrato m
subcontract (v) subcontratar
subcontractor subcontratista m/f
subject asunto m
subject to sujeto(-a) a
sublease (n) subarriendo m
sublease (v) subarrendar
sublet (n) subarrendar
submit (document) presentar
subsidiary (n) filial f
subsidiary company compañía f
   filial/subsidiaria
subsidize subvencionar
subsidy subsidio m, subvención f
subtotal total m parcial
succeed (do well) tener éxito,
   prosperar; (manage to) conseguir
success éxito m
successful con éxito,
   afortunado(-a), próspero(-a)
sue demandar
suitable idóneo(-a), conveniente
sum (of money) cantidad f, suma f
sundries artículos mpl varios
supermarket supermercado m
supervise supervisar
supervision supervisión f, vigilancia f
supervisor supervisor(a)
supervisory de supervisión,
   de control
supplementary suplementario(-a)
supplier suministrador(a),
   proveedor(a), abastecedor(a)
supply (n) (action) oferta f,
   abastecimiento m, suministro m
supply (v)
   suministrar, abastecer, proveer
supply price precio m de oferta
support (v) sostener, apoyar
support price precio m
   de subvención
surcharge sobretasa f, recargo m
surplus excedente m,
   exceso m, superávit m

surrender (n) (insurance) rescate m
surrender value valor m de rescate
survey (n) (examination) inspección f
survey (v) (inspect)
   examinar, inspeccionar
surveyor inspector(a) de obra
suspend suspender
suspension of payments
   suspensión f de pagos
swap (n) intercambio m
swap (v) cambiar, intercambiar
swatch muestra f pequeña
switch over to cambiarse/pasarse a
switchboard centralita f
synergy sinergia f
system sistema m
systems analyst analista m/f
   de sistemas

T

tacit approval aprobación f tácita
take a call recibir una llamada
take action tomar medidas
take legal advice consultar a
   un abogado
take off (deduct, remove) rebajar,
   quitar; (plane) despegar
take on more staff emplear
   más personal
take out a policy hacerse un seguro
take over (from so.) tomar posesión
take place tener lugar
take (so.) to court llevar (a alguien)
   ante los tribunales
take stock hacer un inventario
take the initiative tomar la iniciativa
takeover adquisición f
takeover bid oferta f pública de
   adquisición (OPA)
takeover target objeto m de una OPA
takings ingresos mpl de un negocio
tangible assets activo m tangible
target market mercado m previsto
tariff (price) tarifa f, precio m
tariff bariers barreras fpl arancelarias
task tarea f
tax (n) impuesto m
tax (v) gravar con un impuesto
tax assessment cálculo m de la
   base impositiva
tax collection
   recaudación f de impuestos

tax consultant asesor(a) fiscal

tax credit
crédito *m* por impuestos pagados

tax deducted at source
impuestos *mpl* retenidos en el origen

tax evasion evasión *f* de impuestos, fraude *m* fiscal

tax exemption exención *f* fiscal

tax haven paraíso *m* fiscal

tax inspector
inspector(a) de Hacienda

tax paid impuesto *m* pagado

tax rate tipo *m* impositivo

tax return/declaration declaración *f* de renta

tax year
año *m* fiscal, ejercicio *m* fiscal

tax-deductible desgravable

tax-free libre de impuestos

taxable income renta *f* imponible

taxpayer contribuyente *m/f*

telephone (n) teléfono *m*

telephone (v) telefonear, llamar

telephone directory guía *f* telefónica

telephone line línea *f* telefónica

telephone switchboard
centralita *f* telefónica

telephonist telefonista *m/f*

temp (n) secretario(-a) eventual

temp (v) hacer trabajo eventual

temporary employment
empleo *m* eventual

temporary staff
personal *m* eventual

tenancy *(agreement)*
(contrato *m* de) arrendamiento *m*

tenant
inquilino(-a), arrendatario(-a)

tender (n) *(offer to work)* oferta *f*

term *(time of validity)* plazo *m*

term loan préstamo *m* a plazo fijo

terminal (adj) terminal

terminate terminar

terminate an agreement poner término a un acuerdo

termination clause
cláusula *f* resolutoria

terms condiciones *fpl*, términos *mpl*

terms of employment
condiciones *fpl* de servicio

territory *(of salesman)* territorio *m*

tertiary industry industria *f* terciaria

test (n)
examen *m*, ensayo *m*, prueba *f*

test (v) probar, someter a prueba

theft robo *m*

third party tercero *m*

third quarter tercer trimestre *m*

threshold price precio *m* umbral

throughput rendimiento *m*

tie-up *(link)* conexión *f*

tighten up on intensificar (el control)

time, on a tiempo

timetable (n) *(appointments)*
programa *m*, calendario *m*; *(trains, etc.)* horario *m*

timetable (v)
preparar un horario, programar

tip (n) *(money)* propina *f*

tip (v) *(give money)* dar una propina

token charge precio *m* simbólico

toll peaje *m*

toll free a cobro revertido

ton tonelada *f*

tonnage tonelaje *m*

tool herramienta *f*, instrumento *m*

top management alta dirección *f*

top quality alta calidad *f*, calidad superior

total (adj) total

total (n) total *m*, totalidad *f*

total (v) totalizar, sumar

total amount cantidad *f* total

total cost coste *m* total

total invoice value valor *m* total de factura

track record antecedentes *mpl*

trade (n) *(business)* comercio *m*

trade (v) comerciar, negociar

trade deficit/gap
déficit *m* comercial

trade directory
repertorio *m*, guía *f* comercial

trade discount/terms descuento *m* para comerciantes del sector

trade fair feria *f* comercial

trade journal
revista *f* profesional especializada

trade price precio *m* al por mayor

trade union sindicato *m*

trade unionist sindicalista *m/f*

trademark/trade name
marca *f* comercial

trader comerciante *m/f*

trading loss pérdida *f* de ejercicio

trading partner empresa *f* que comercia con otra
trading profit beneficio *m* de ejercicio, beneficios *mpl* de explotación
train (n) tren *m*
train (v) *(learn)* prepararse, formarse; *(teach)* preparar, capacitar, formar
trainee aprendiz(a)
transaction transacción *f*
transfer (n) traslado *m*, transferencia *f*, transbordo *m*
transfer of funds transferencia *f* de fondos
transit tránsito *m*
transit lounge sala *f* de tránsito
transit visa visado *m* de tránsito
translation traducción *f*
transport (n) transporte *m*
transport (v) transportar, llevar
trial period periodo *m* de prueba
trial sample muestra *f*
tribunal juzgado *m*
triplicate, in por triplicado
true copy compulsa *f*, copia *f* exacta
turn down rechazar
turn over (v) *(make sales)* tener un volumen de ventas de
turnkey operation operación *f* llaves en mano
turnover *(sales)* volumen *m* de ventas, cifra *f* de negocios

U

unaudited accounts cuentas *fpl* sin verificar
unauthorized expenditure gastos *mpl* no autorizados
unavailable no disponible, inasequible
unconditional incondicional, sin condiciones
undated sin fecha
under *(according to)* conforme a; *(less than)* por debajo de, menos de
under contract bajo contrato
under new management cambio *m* de dirección
undercharge cobrar de menos
undercut a rival vender a precio más bajo que un rival
undersell vender más barato
undersigned abajo firmante *m/f*

understanding acuerdo *m*, arreglo *m*
undertaking *(company)* empresa *f*; *(promise)* compromiso *m*, promesa *f*
underwrite *(guarantee)* avalar
unemployed parado(-a), desempleado(-a), en paro
unemployment paro *m*, desempleo *m*
unfair competition competencia *f* desleal
unfulfilled order pedido *m* no servido/por servir
unilateral unilateral
union sindicato *m*
unique selling point/proposition (USP) argumento *m* de venta
unit cost coste *m* unitario/por unidad
unit price precio *m* por unidad
unload *(goods)* descargar
unobtainable inalcanzable, imposible de conseguir
unofficial extraoficial, no oficial, oficioso(-a)
unpaid invoices facturas *fpl* impagadas
unsecured creditor acreedor(a) común/sin garantía
unsuccessful fracasado(-a), sin éxito
up front por adelantado
up to date *(complete)* al día; *(modern)* actual, moderno(-a)
up-market de primera calidad
update (v) actualizar, poner al día, modernizar
urgent urgente
use (n) uso *m*, empleo *m*
use (v) emplear, usar, utilizar
user-friendly de fácil uso
utilization utilización *f*, uso *m*, empleo *m*

V

vacancy *(for job)* plaza *f*, vacante *f*
valid válido(-a)
valuation valoración *f*, evaluación *f*, tasación *f*
value (n) valor *m*
value (v) valorar, tasar, evaluar
value added tax (VAT) impuesto *m* sobre el valor añadido (IVA)

variable costs

variable costs costes *mpl* variables
VAT invoice factura *f* con el IVA
vendor vendedor(a)
venture capital capital-riesgo *m*
verbal agreement acuerdo *m* verbal
verification verificación *f*
verify verificar
vested interest interés *m* personal, intereses *mpl* creados
veto a decision vetar una decisión
visa visado *m*
visible trade comercio *m* de visibles
void (adj) *(not valid)* nulo(-a), inválido(-a)
void (v) invalidar
volume discount descuento *m* por volumen
volume of business volumen de negocios
volume of trade volumen *m* comercial
voluntary liquidation liquidación *f* voluntaria
vote of thanks voto *m* de gracias
voucher bono *m*, vale *m*

W

wage sueldo *m*, salario *m*
wage negotiations negociaciones *fpl* salariales
waiting period periodo *m* de espera
waive renunciar, desistir
waiver clause cláusula *f* de renuncia
wallet cartera *f*
warehouse (n) almacén *m*
warehouse (v) almacenar
warehousing almacenaje *m*
warrant (n) *(document)* autorización *f* legal, orden *f*
warrant (v) *(guarantee)* garantizar
warranty (n) garantía *f*
wastage pérdida *f*, desperdicio *m*
waste (n) desperdicio *m*, desecho *m*, residuos *mpl*
waste (v) *(use too much)* desperdiciar, malgastar
waybill carta *f* de porte
wear and tear desgaste *m* natural/normal
weekly semanalmente
weigh pesar

weight peso *m*
weighted index índice *m* ponderado
whole-life insurance seguro *m* corriente de vida
wholesale (adv) al por mayor
wholesale discount descuento *m* al por mayor
wholesaler mayorista *m/f*
win a contract conseguir un contrato
wind up *(a company)* liquidar
window display escaparate *m*
withdraw *(an offer)* retirar
witness (n) testimonio *m*, testigo *m/f*
witness (v) *(a document)* firmar como testigo
word-processing tratamiento *m* de textos
work (v) trabajar
work in progress trabajo *m* en curso
work permit permiso *m* de trabajo
working conditions condiciones *fpl* de trabajo
working day jornada *f*
worldwide (adj) mundial, global
worth, be valer
wrap up *(goods)* embalar, empaquetar
writ orden *f*, mandato *m*, mandamiento *m*
write escribir
write down *(assets)* depreciar el valor de un activo
write off *(debt)* anular, cancelar, eliminar
write out a cheque/check extender un cheque
write-off *(loss)* deuda *f* incobrable, pérdida *f* total
written agreement acuerdo por escrito

X, Y, Z

yearbook anuario *m*
yearly payment pago *m* anual
yellow pages páginas *fpl* amarillas
yield (n) *(on investment)* rendimiento *m*, rédito *m*
yield (v) rendir, devengar
zip code código *m* postal

Spanish–English Business Dictionary

f	**feminine**
m	**masculine**
pl	**plural**
(adj)	**adjective**
(n)	**noun**
(v)	**verb**
so.	**someone**
sth.	**something**

A

abajo firmante *m/f* undersigned
abandono *m* **de responsabilidad** disclaimer
abastecedor(a) supplier
abastecer cater for, supply
abastecimiento *m* supply
abierto(-a) open (adj) *(not closed)*
abogado(-a) lawyer, solicitor
abogado defensor defence counsel
abonar pay out; credit
abono *m* credit entry; season ticket
abordar board, go on board
abrir la sesión open a meeting
abrir un negocio open/start new business
abrir una carta de crédito issue a letter of credit
abrir una cuenta bancaria open a bank account
abrir una línea de crédito open a line of credit
acabar complete, finish
acaparar capture
acaparar el mercado corner the market
acarreo *m* **del transporte** haulage costs, haulage rates
accesible available
acceso *m* entry *(going in)*
accidente *m* **laboral** industrial accident
acción *f* share/stock *(in a company)*
acciones ordinarias ordinary shares, equities, securities
accionista *m/f* shareholder
accionista importante major shareholder

aceptar accept
aceptar hacer algo agree to do sth.
aceptar la entrega de mercancías accept delivery of a shipment
aceptar la responsabilidad de algo accept liability for sth.
acogida *f* reception, welcome, acceptance
aconsejar recommend, advise
acordar agree, approve
acreditar credit
acreedor(a) creditor
acreedor común/sin garantía unsecured creditor
acreedor con garantía secured creditor
acreedor diferido deferred creditor
acta *f* minutes *(of meeting)*
acta notarial affidavit
activo *m* asset
activo circulante current assets
activo congelado frozen assets
activo neto net assets, net worth
activo realizable liquid assets
actual present, up to date, modern
actualizar update
acuerdo *m* agreement, understanding; compromise; deal
acuerdo a tanto alzado fixed-price agreement
acuerdo por escrito written agreement
acumular stock up
acumularse accrue
acumulativo(-a) cumulative
acusado(-a) accused (n), defendant
acusar recibo de una carta acknowledge receipt of a letter
adelantado, por up front
además de further to
adeudar en cuenta debit an account
adeudarse run into debt
adjudicar un contrato a alguien award a contract to so.
adjuntar enclose
adjunto(-a) deputy, assistant
admisible acceptable
adquirir buy, acquire
adquisición *f* takeover, acquisition
aduana *f* customs
aduanero(-a) customs official
afiliado(-a) associate (adj)

afortunado(-a) successful

agencia de cambio bureau de change

agencia de cobro de morosos debt collection agency

agencia de publicidad advertising agency

agenda f appointments book

agente m/f agent

agente de bolsa stockbroker

agente en exclusiva sole agent

agente de, ser represent

agotado(-a) out of stock

agotar las existencias run out of stock

agrupar batch; consolidate (shipments)

aguas territoriales, en offshore

ahorrar save

ahorra energía, que energy-saving

ahorro m saving

ajustado(-a) al coste de la vida index-linked

ajustar reconcile

ajuste m adjustment

ajuste fino fine tuning

albarán m delivery note, invoice

alcanzar una meta meet a target

almacén m warehouse, store, storeroom

almacén frigorífico cold store

almacenaje m warehousing; computer storage

almacenamiento m storage

almacenar store, warehouse; stock (goods)

almuerzo m **de negocios** business lunch

alquilar rent, hire

alquilar un coche hire/rent a car

alquilar una oficina let an office

alquiler m rent

alta dirección top management

alza f rise, increase

amo m owner, boss

amortización f amortization; redemption (of a loan)

amparo m **fiscal** tax shelter

ampliación f extension

ampliar expand

análisis estadístico statistical analysis

anaquel m shelf

anexo m appendix

anotación f entry

anotar note, record (v)

anotar una contrapartida/un contrasiento contra an entry

antecedentes mpl track record

antedatar backdate

anteproyecto m draft plan

anticipar advance

anticipo m advance

anticipo a cuenta advance on account

anticipo de caja a cuenta cash advance

anticuado(-a) out of date, old-fashioned, obsolete

anualmente annually

anuario m directory, yearbook

anular cancel, invalidate; write off (debt)

anular un acuerdo call off a deal

anular un contrato cancel a contract

anunciante m/f advertiser

anunciar un nuevo producto advertise a new product

anunciar una vacante advertise a vacancy

anuncio m advertisement; commercial (TV)

anuncios por palabras classified advertisements

añadir el 10% por el servicio add on 10% for service

año m year

año civil calendar year

año fiscal financial year, tax year

año, al per annum, per year

apalancamiento m **financiero** gearing, leverage

apartado m **de correos** box number

apelación f appeal (against a decision)

apelar appeal (against a decision)

aplazamiento m postponement, deferment

aplazar postpone, defer

aplazar una reunión adjourn a meeting

apoderado(-a) lawyer, attorney; nominee, proxy

apoyar back up, support

apreciar appreciate

apremiar chase (an order)

aprender learn

aprendiz(a) trainee

aprobación f **tácita** tacit approval
aprobar approve, agree (in a vote)
apropiar convert
aprovechar capitalize on, take advantage of
aptitud f capacity, ability
apuntar note, point out
arancel m duty, tariff
arbitrar un litigio (en una disputa) arbitrate (in a dispute)
archivador(a) filing cabinet
archivar back up, save (computer file)
archivar documentos file documents
archivo m computer file; document file
archivos mpl records
arreglar fix, mend
arreglárselas manage to
arreglo m agreement, understanding
arrendador(a) lessor
arrendamiento m lease; rent
arrendamiento financiero leasing
arrendar let, lease; rent
arrendar equipo lease/hire (out) equipment
arrendatario(-a) lessee, tenant
arriendo m lease
arriendo, ceder en let, lease (of landlord)
arriendo, tomar en rent, lease (of tenant)
arriesgado(-a) risky
arriesgar risk (money)
arruinar bankrupt (v)
artículo m article, item
artículo de reclamo loss-leader
artículos con desperfectos seconds
artículos de fácil venta fast-selling items
artículos varios sundries
asamblea f **de personal** staff meeting
ascender promote (give better job)
ascender a amount to
ascenso m promotion (to better job)
ascensor m lift
asegurador(a) insurer
asegurar insure
asequible obtainable
asesor(a) consultant
asesor(a) fiscal tax consultant
asesoramiento jurídico legal advice
asesoría f consultancy firm

asiento m entry
asiento de débito/adeudo debit entry
asignar fondos fund (v)
asignar fondos a un proyecto commit funds to a project
asistir attend (meeting); assist, help
asistir, no miss
asociado(-a) associate (adj); partner (n)
aspirar a aim
asunto m matter, subject
asunto problemático problem area
asuntos de negocios, por on business
atasco m bottleneck
atender a cater for, serve
atender una demanda meet a demand
aterrizar land (of plane)
atracar berth
atracar dock (ship)
atraer appeal to, attract
atrasado(-a) overdue
atrasos mpl arrears
audiencia f court
auditor(a) auditor
auditoría f audit
aumentar mark up, increase, raise (price)
aumentar appreciate
aumento m increase
aumento de salario/de sueldo annual pay rise
ausente absent
autoedición f desk-top publishing
autónomo(-a) self-employed
autoridad f authority
autorización f authorization
autorización legal warrant
autorizar license; entitle
autorizar el pago authorize payment
auxiliar m/f assistant
auxiliar administrativo(-a) junior clerk
aval guarantee, warranty
avalar underwrite, guarantee
avería f average (insurance); breakdown (machine)
averiarse break down (of machine)
avión m plane
avión de carga freight plane
avisar notify
ayudante m/f assistant
ayudar assist, help

baja

B

baja f drop
bajar decrease, reduce, drop
bajo contrato under contract
balance m balance
balanza f **comercial** balance of trade
bancarrota f bankruptcy
banco m bank
banco comercial clearing bank
banco de negocios/banco mercantil merchant bank
bandeja f pallet
barato(-a) cheap
barco m ship
barreras fpl **arancelarias** tariff barriers
base f **de datos** database
beneficiario(-a) beneficiary, payee
beneficiarse de benefit from
beneficio m profit
beneficio bruto gross profit
beneficio neto net profit
beneficio sobre el papel paper profit
beneficios mpl earnings, trading profit
beneficios de la empresa corporate profits
beneficios netos de impuestos after-tax profit
beneficioso(-a) cost-effective
bienes mpl **de consumo** consumer goods
bienes de equipo capital equipment
bienes raíces real estate
billete m fare
billete abierto open ticket
billete de banco banknote
billete en lista de espera standby ticket
bloquear block
bodega f hold (ship)
bolsa f stock exchange; stock market
bolsa de comercio/de contratación commodity market, commodity exchange
bonificación f bonus; discount
bono m debenture; government bond; voucher
bonos-basura mpl junk bonds
borrador m draft, rough plan
buen precio good value (for money)
buena calidad good quality

buena compra good buy
buque m ship
burocracia f red tape

C

caber contain, hold (v)
caducado(-a) out of date
caducar expire; lapse
caducidad f expiry; obsolescence
caer drop
caída f drop
caja f case (box); cash desk; checkout (in supermarket)
caja fuerte/caja de caudales safe
cajero(-a) cashier
cajero automático cash dispenser, ATM
calculadora f calculator
calcular calculate, estimate
calcular mal miscalculate
calcular un precio quote, estimate costs
cálculo m calculation, estimate
cálculo de la base impositiva tax assessment
calendario m calendar, timetable
calidad, alta top quality
calidad superior, de high-quality
calidad, de primera up-market
callejero m street directory
Cámara f **de Comercio** Chamber of Commerce
cambiar change; swap, exchange; convert, alter
cambiar de dueño change hands
cambiar divisas exchange (v) currency
cambiarse a switch over to
cambio m change, cash; difference
cambio de dirección under new management
cambio fijo fixed exchange rate
camión m **de carga pesada** heavy goods vehicle
campaña f **de ventas** sales campaign
cancelación f **de una cita** cancellation of an appointment
cancelar cancel; write off (debt)
canje m **parcial** part exchange
canjear exchange (one thing for another)
canon m **de autor** royalty

cantidad f amount, quantity; figure; sum *(of money)*
capacitar train, teach
capital m **en acciones** equity capital
capital-riesgo m risk capital, venture capital
carestía f cost of living
carga f cargo; shipment
carga aérea air freight
carga perecedera perishable cargo
cargar load *(computer program; truck, ship)*
cargar en cuenta debit an account
cargar en exceso overcharge (v)
cargar una compra en cuenta charge a purchase
cargo m charge; position, job; job title
cargo de, hacerse take over *(from so.)*
cargos adicionales additional charges
caro(-a) dear, expensive
carretera f road
carretilla f **elevadora de horquilla** fork-lift truck
carta f letter
carta adjunta enclosure
carta certificada registered letter
carta de crédito letter of credit
carta de porte waybill
carta de reclamación letter of complaint
carta de recomendación letter of reference
carta de reiteración follow-up letter
carta explicatoria covering letter
cartera f briefcase, wallet; portfolio
casa f **comercial** firm
casa matriz parent company
casa, de la in-house
cash flow actualizado discounted cash flow
catalogar catalogue/catalog, index
catálogo m catalogue/catalog, list
catálogo de ventas por correo mail-order catalogue/catalog
categoría f category, class
causa de, a owing to
ceder en arriendo lease (v) *(of landlord)*
celebrar una reunión hold a meeting
censor(a) auditor

centralita f *(telephone)* switchboard
centralización f **de las compras** central purchasing
centro comercial shopping centre/center
centro de beneficios profit centre/center
centro de reparaciones service centre/center
cercano(-a) close to
cero m nil, zero
cerrado(-a) closed
cerradura f lock
cerrar close down
cerrar con llave lock (v)
cerrar un trato clinch
cerrar una cuenta close an account
cerrar una tienda lock up a shop
certificado de aprobación certificate of approval
certificado de una acción share/stock certificate
certificar certify; register *(letter)*
cesar stop *(doing sth.)*
cesión-arrendamiento f lease-back
cheque m cheque/check
cheque conformado certified cheque/check
cheque de sueldo/de salario pay cheque/check
cheque en blanco blank cheque/check
chequeo m **al azar** random check
cíclico(-a) cyclical
ciclo m cycle
cierre m closing
cifra f figure
cifra de negocios turnover *(sales)*
cifras reales actuals
cita f appointment, meeting
claro(-a) clear (adj) *(easy to understand)*
clase f **preferente** business class
clasificación f rating
clasificador m card index, filing cabinet
clasificar classify; index
cláusula f article, clause
cláusula de excepción escape clause
cláusula de renuncia waiver clause
cláusula de rescisión cancellation clause

cláusula penal

cláusula penal penalty clause
cláusula resolutoria
  termination clause
clausurar close
cliente *m/f* client, customer
cliente habitual regular customer
cobertura *f* insurance cover
cobrador(a) collector
cobrar charge *(money)*
cobrar de más overcharge (v)
cobrar de menos undercharge
cobrar un cheque cash a
  cheque/check
cobrar una deuda collect a debt
cobro *m* **a la entrega, contra**
  reembolso cash on delivery (c.o.d.)
cobro de morosos debt collection
cobro revertido, a toll free
código *m* **de barras** bar code
código postal/territorial postcode,
  zip code, area code
codirector(a) gerente
  joint managing director
coeficiente *m* factor *(influence)*; rate
coeficiente de amortización/
  depreciación depreciation rate
coincidir agree *(be same as)*
coma *f* **decimal** decimal point
comenzar begin, start
comercialización *f*
  merchandizing, marketing
comercializar un producto
  merchandize a product
comerciante *m/f* trader, merchant
comerciante al por mayor
  wholesaler
comerciar handle, deal in, sell
comercio *m* commerce,
  trade; business
comercio de visibles visible trade
comercio exterior external trade,
  overseas trade
comisión *f* commission
comisión de arbitraje
  arbitration board
comisionista *m/f* factor
cómodo(-a) convenient
compañía *f* company
compañía de seguros
  insurance company
comparar (con) compare (with)
comparar precios shop around,
  compare prices

compartir share *(use with so.)*
compensación *f* **por daños y**
  perjuicios compensation
  for damage
compensar compensate, make up for
competencia *f* **desleal**
  unfair competition
competencia dura stiff competition
competente qualified, skilled
competidor(a) competitor
competitividad *f* competitiveness
competitivo(-a) competing (adj)
competitivo, con precio
  competitively priced
completar complete
completo(-a) complete (adj)
compra *f* purchase
compra a granel bulk buying
compra a plazos hire purchase (HP)
compra al contado cash purchase,
  spot purchase
compra de futuros forward buying
comprador(a) buyer, purchaser
comprar buy, purchase
comprar a futuros buy forward
comprobación *f* check, examination
comprobante *m* counterfoil
comprobar check, examine
compromiso *m* obligation, duty;
  appointment; undertaking
compromisos *mpl* commitments
compulsa *f* true copy, certified copy
común(a) common
comunicaciones *fpl* communications
comunicado *m* **de prensa**
  press release
comunicar communicate;
  be engaged
comunicarse communicate
conceder una licencia license
concertación *f*
  harmonization; reconciliation
concesión *f* franchise
concesionario(-a) franchisee
conciliación *f* compromise
concluir conclude; complete
conclusión *f* conclusion, end;
  condition, state
condición jurídica legal status
condición, sin unconditional
condicional conditional
condiciones *fpl* terms

condiciones de servicio
terms of employment
condiciones de trabajo
working conditions
condiciones de venta
conditions/terms of sale
conexión f interface; port *(computer)*;
tie-up, link
confeccionar make out *(invoice)*
conferencia f **de prensa**
press conference
confianza, de reliable
confidencial confidential
confiscación f forfeiture
confiscar seize
conflictos laborales labour/
labor disputes
conforme a according to, under
congelación f **de créditos**
credit freeze
congelar freeze *(prices)*
conjunto(-a) joint
conjunto, en altogether, overall
conocido(-a) well-known
conocimiento m **de embarque**
bill of lading
conseguir get, obtain;
manage to, succeed
conseguir fondos secure funds,
raise money
conseguir un contrato win a contract
consejero(-a) director; consultant
consejo m board of directors
conservación f maintenance
consigna f left luggage office
consignación f consignment
consignar dispatch, send, ship
consolidación f **de un préstamo**
restructuring of a loan
consolidar establish
consorcio m consortium
constar de consist of
constituir en sociedad incorporate,
set up *(a company)*
consultar a un abogado
take legal advice
consultoría f consultancy firm
consumidor(a) consumer (n)
contabilidad f
accounts, bookkeeping
contable m/f bookkeeper, accountant
contactar contact
contenedor m container *(shipping)*

contener contain
contenido m contents
contestación f reply, answer
contestador m **automático**
answering machine
contestar reply, answer
continuamente continually
continuar continue
continuo(-a) constant,
continual, continuous
contra reembolso on delivery
contraasiento m contra entry
contrabando m smuggling
contraer deudas incur debts
contraoferta f counter-offer
contrapartida f contra entry
contrario(-a) contrary (adj)
contratar contract
contratar personal hire staff
contratista m/f contractor
contrato m contract
contrato a tanto alzado
fixed-price agreement
contrato de arrendamiento tenancy
contrato de Bolsa contract note
contrato de empleo
contract of employment
contrato de venta bill of sale
contrato en exclusiva
exclusive agreement
contrato, por contractually
contribuyente m/f taxpayer
control m check, examination;
control, power
control de existencias stock control,
inventory control
control de precios price controls
control presupuestario
budgetary control
control, de supervisory
controlar monitor
controlar un negocio
control a business
conveniente convenient, suitable
convenio m agreement, covenant
convenir agree, approve; convert
convocar convene
copia f copy, duplicate *(of document)*
copia de reserva/de seguridad
backup copy
copia exacta/certificada true copy,
certified copy
copia impresa computer printout

copiar

copiar copy, duplicate
correcto(-a) correct, right
corredor(a) de bolsa stockbroker
corredor(a) de seguros
  insurance broker
corregir correct
correo *m* post, mail
correo aéreo airmail
correo electrónico electronic mail
correspondencia *f*
  correspondence, mail
correspondencia de salida
  outgoing mail
corresponder agree *(be same as)*
corresponder a algo
  correspond with sth.
corriente normal, common, frequent,
  ordinary; current
costar cost (v)
costas *fpl* judiciales (legal) costs,
  legal charges
coste *m* cost
coste, seguro y flete
  cost, insurance and freight
coste de almacenaje storage *(cost)*
coste de la gestión de deudas
  factoring charges
coste de producción prime cost
coste de vida cost of living
coste del transporte haulage costs,
  haulage rates
coste descargado landed costs
coste unitario/por unidad unit cost
costes de envío shipping charges,
  shipping costs
costes de puesta en marcha
  start-up costs
costes fijos fixed costs
costo *m* cost
costo más honorarios cost plus
costoso(-a) dear, expensive
cotejar check, compare
cotización *f* price, quote, quotation
cotizar pay, contribute; quote, price
crear una compañía
  set up a company
crecer expand, grow
crecimiento *m* growth
crédito *m* credit
crédito a corto plazo short credit
crédito a largo plazo extended credit,
  long credit
crédito abierto open credit

crédito por impuestos pagados
  tax credit
crédito renovable revolving credit
crédito, a on credit, on account
crónico(-a) chronic
cruzar un cheque cross a
  cheque/check
cuadrar reconcile, balance
cualificado(-a) qualified, skilled
cuanto a, en regarding
cuarto *m*/cuarta parte *f*
  quarter *(25%)*
cuarto trimestre fourth quarter
cubierta *f* cover *(top)*
cubrir gastos break even, cover costs
cubrir un puesto fill a post
cubrir un riesgo cover a risk
cuenta *f* account; bill *(in a restaurant)*
cuenta abierta open account
cuenta bancaria bank account
cuenta bloqueada frozen account
cuenta compensada contra account
cuenta conjunta joint account
cuenta corriente current account
cuenta de ahorro savings account
cuenta de depósito/a plazo
  deposit account
cuenta de gastos de representación
  expense account
cuenta de pérdidas y ganancias
  profit and loss account
cuenta detallada detailed account,
  itemized account
cuenta en descubierto
  overdrawn account
cuenta en participación joint account
cuenta inactiva dead account
cuenta presupuestaria budget
  account *(in bank)*
cuenta, a on account
cuentas a, por cobrar accounts
  receivable, bills receivable
cuentas a, por pagar accounts
  payable, bills payable
cuentas sin verificar
  unaudited accounts
cuestión *f* matter *(for discussion)*
cumplidor(a) reliable
cumplir meet, satisfy
cumplir un objetivo meet a target
cumplir un plazo establecido meet
  a deadline
cumplir una promesa keep a promise

cuota f fee
cuota de depreciación
allowance for depreciation
cuota de importación import quota
cuota de inscripción registration fee
cuota de mercado market share
cupo m quota
cupón de anuncio coupon ad
cursar un pedido place an order
curso m **de gestión empresarial**
management course
curso de iniciación induction course

D

dañar damage
daño m damage
daños causados por incendio
fire damage
daños y perjuicios damages
DAO CAD (computer assisted design)
dar yield (interest)
dar una propina tip, give a tip
darse cuenta realize (understand)
darse prisa hurry up
datos mpl data
debajo de, por under, less than
debate m discussion
debe m debit
deber owe
debido(-a) due (to), owing (to)
débil slack, weak
débito m debit
decidir decide, rule
decisión f ruling
decisión, tomar una reach a decision
declaración f declaration, return
declaración de aduana
customs declaration
declaración de ingresos nulos
nil return
declaración de renta tax return
decomiso m forfeiture
decreciente decreasing (adj)
decretar rule
deducción f deduction
deducciones personales
personal allowances
deducible deductible
deducir deduct
defecto m defect
defecto, en su failing that
defectuoso(-a) defective, faulty

defenderse en juicio defend a lawsuit
defensor(a) del pueblo ombudsman
déficit m **comercial** trade deficit,
trade gap
dejar stop (doing sth.)
delegado(-a) deputy; delegate
delegado(-a) sindical(-a)
shop steward
demanda f demand (need); claim
demanda estacional
seasonal demand
demanda por daños y perjuicios
action for damages
demandado(-a) defendant
demandante m/f plaintiff
demandar sue
demora f delay
demorar delay
demostrar demonstrate, show
departamento m department (in
office); division (in company)
departamento de contabilidad
accounts department
depender de depend on, rely on
dependiente(-a) shop assistant
depositante m/f depositor
depositar deposit
depósito m down payment; store;
storage; deposit (paid in advance),
down payment; bank deposit
depósito a plazo time deposit
depósito (no) reembolsable
(non-)refundable deposit
depreciación f depreciation, loss
of value
depreciar el valor de un activo
write down (assets)
depreciarse depreciate, lose value
derecho(-a) right (adj) (not left)
derecho m right, law, entitlement
derecho de ocupación security
of tenure
derecho de paso right of way
derecho de retención lien
derecho mercantil commercial law
derecho a, dar entitle
derechos mpl fee (for admission)
derechos de aduana customs duty
derechos de autor royalty
derechos de importación import duty
derivar de result from
derrumbamiento m collapse
derrumbarse collapse

desarrollar

desarrollar develop
desarrollo m development, growth
descargar unload *(goods)*
descender drop, fall
descenso m downturn; decrease
descontar discount; deduct
descripción f **del puesto de trabajo**
job description
descubierto m overdraft
descuento m discount
descuento al por mayor
wholesale discount
descuento para comerciantes del
sector trade discount, trade terms
descuento por cantidad
quantity discount
descuento por pago al contado
cash discount
desechable disposable
desecho m waste
desembolsar pay out
desembolso m expenditure, outlay
desembolsos outgoings
desempleado(-a) unemployed
desempleo m
unemployment; redundancy
desgaste m **natural/normal**
wear and tear
desglosar break down, itemize
desglose m breakdown *(items)*
desgravable tax-deductible
deshacerse de algo dispose of,
get rid of sth.
desistir waive
desistir de una acción
abandon an action
despachar dispatch, send, ship
despachar pedidos atrasados
release dues
despachar un pedido fulfil an order
despacho m office; dispatch, sending
despacho aduanero/de aduanas
customs clearance
despacho de pedidos
order fulfilment
despedido, ser get the sack,
be dismissed
despedir a alguien sack so.
despedir a un empleado dismiss
an employee
despedir por falta de trabajo lay off,
make redundant
despegar take off *(plane)*

desperdiciar waste, use too much of
desperdicio m wastage, waste
despido m dismissal, redundancy
destacado(-a)
outstanding, exceptional
destino m destination
destreza f skill
detallada, factura detailed account
detallar break down *(itemize)*
detalle m detail; breakdown *(items)*
detalles details, particulars
detallista m/f retailer
detener el pago de un cheque stop a
cheque/check
deuda f debt
deuda incobrable bad debt,
irrecoverable debt, write-off
deuda morosa
bad debt, outstanding debt
deudas a largo plazo
long-term debts
deudas pendientes
outstanding debts
deudor(a) debtor, defaulter
deudor(a) judicial judgment debtor
devengar
bear, yield *(interest)*; accrue
devolución f refund, return
devolver pay back, refund, repay
devolver por falta de fondos bounce
(cheque/check)
devolver una carta al remitente
return a letter to sender
día m **festivo** bank holiday
día, al every day; per day; up to date
día, poner al update, bring up to date
diagrama m **de flujo** flow chart,
flow diagram
diferencia f difference, discrepancy
diferir differ
diferir el pago defer payment
dimitir resign
dinero m money
dinero efectivo cash
dinero en mano spot cash
dinero suelto change, cash
dique m dock
dirección f management; board of
directors; address
dirección comercial
business address
dirección postal
accommodation address

directo(-a) direct (adj)
director(a) director
director(a) comercial/de ventas
sales manager
director(a) en funciones
acting manager
director(a) gerente
managing director (MD)
directorio m directory
directorio comercial
classified directory
directriz f guideline
dirigir direct, run, manage; operate
dirigir a address (v) *(a letter, parcel)*
dirigir un negocio control a business
disco m **duro** hard disk
discrepancia f discrepancy
discusión, tener una
hold a discussion
discutir discuss
diseñar design
diseño m design
diseño asistido por ordenador
computer assisted design (CAD)
disminución f **de valor** decrease
in value
disminuir decrease, reduce
dispensado(-a) exempt (adj)
dispensar exempt
disponibilidad f availability
disponible available; vacant
disponible, no unavailable
disposición f arrangement
disposiciones fpl
provisions, conditions
disquetera f disk drive
distinto, ser differ, be different
distribuidor(a) distributor; stockist
distribuir distribute, deliver *(goods)*
dividir divide
divisas fpl
foreign currency *(exchange)*
divulgar
release, make public; publicize
doble imposición double taxation
docena f dozen
documento m **adjunto** enclosure
documento escrito instrument
dólar m dollar
domiciliación f **bancaria** direct debit
domicilio m **particular** home address
domicilio social
registered office, headquarters

dueño m/**dueña** f owner, proprietor
duplicado m duplicate
duplicar copy, duplicate
duplicarse double, duplicate

E

echar al correo post, mail (v)
economía f **sumergida**
black economy
economías de escala
economies of scale
económico(-a) economical
ecu/ECU m ecu, ECU (European
currency unit)
edad f **de jubilación** retirement age
edificio m building,
premises, property
edificio principal main building
efectivo m (ready) cash
efecto m effect; instrument
(document)
efecto indirecto spinoff
efectos bills, securities, assets
efectos a cobrar receivables
efectuar effect
eficacia f efficiency; effectiveness
eficaz efficient
eficiencia f effectiveness; efficiency
ejecución f
execution, implementation
ejecutivo(-a) executive (adj/n)
ejecutivo(-a) en formación
management trainee
ejecutivo(-a) de ventas
sales executive
ejercer derecho de opción exercise
an option
ejercicio m **del derecho de opción**
exercise of an option
ejercicio económico/fiscal financial
year, tax year
elaborar process, deal with
elegir choose
elemento m element,
factor *(influence)*
eliminar eliminate, write off *(debt)*
embalador(a) packer
embalaje m packing *(material)*
embalaje hermético
airtight packaging
embalaje vacío/ficticio dummy pack
embalar pack, wrap up *(goods)*

embarcar

embarcar embark
embarcarse board, go on board
embargar embargo; seize
embargo m embargo; seizure
embotellamiento m bottleneck
emisión f **de acciones gratuitas**
  scrip issue
emisión de derechos rights issue
emisión publicitaria commercial (TV)
emolumentos mpl fee (for services)
empaquetador(-a) packer
empaquetar pack; wrap up (goods)
empezar begin, start
empleado(-a) employee
empleado(-a) de oficina clerk
emplear employ
empleo m appointment, job,
  employment; utilization, use
empleo eventual
  temporary employment
empleo, sin out of work
emprender un negocio open/start a
  new business
empresa f business, firm, enterprise
empresa conjunta joint venture
empresa de transportes carrier,
  haulage/transport company
empresa mediana
  middle-sized company
empresarial entrepreneurial
empresario(-a) employer,
  businessman, businesswoman
empréstito m loan capital
encargado(-a) manager (of
  branch, shop)
encargar order (goods)
encargarse de deal with
encarte m **publicitario**
  magazine insert
enchufe m contact; electric plug
encontrar, no miss, not to meet
encontrarse meet (so.)
encuesta f opinion poll
endémico(-a) chronic
endeudado(-a) indebted
endeudarse get into debt
endoso m endorsement
enlace m link
enmendar amend
enmienda f amendment
ensayo m test
entablar enter into

entrada f entry (going in); down
  payment, deposit
entradas fpl receipts
entrar en enter, go in
entrar en dársena dock (ship)
entrega f delivery (goods)
entrega gratuita free delivery
entrega urgente express delivery
entregar hand over, deliver
entrevista f interview (for a job)
entrevistar interview (for a job)
envasar pack
envase m container
enviar dispatch, send, ship, forward
enviar por carga aérea airfreight (v)
enviar por correo post (v)
envío m shipment, consignment;
  dispatch, sending; shipping;
  remittance
envolver wrap (up)
equilibrar balance (a budget)
equipaje m luggage, baggage
equipar equip
equipo m equipment
equipo directivo management team
equitativo(-a) fair
equivocación f error, mistake
errar miss
error m error, slip, mistake
error aleatorio random error
error de cálculo miscalculation
error de ordenador computer error
escala, a pequeña small-scale
escalonar stagger
escaparate m shop window
escasez f shortage
escaso(-a) short of
escribir write, correspond
escrito(-a) a mano handwritten
escritorio m desk
escritura f deed
escuela f **de empresariales**
  business school
escuela de secretariado
  secretarial college
espacio m room, space
espacio publicitario
  advertising space
esperar instrucciones
  await instructions
estabilidad f stability
estabilizarse level off, level out
establecer establish

establecimiento *m* establishment

estación *f* season; rail station

estadísticas *fpl* statistics

estado *m* state

estado de cuenta bank balance

estado de cuenta mensual
monthly statement

estafa *f* fraud

estándar standard (adj)

estandarizar standardize

estantería *f* shelving, shelf

estantería display stand

estimación *f* estimate

estimar estimate

estimular stimulate,
promote, encourage

estímulo *m* incentive

estipulación *f* provision, condition

estipular stipulate

estrategia *f* **comercial**
business strategy

estropearse break down *(of machine)*

estudio *m* **de mercado**
market research

etiqueta *f* label

etiqueta de precio price label,
price tag

etiquetar label

evadir impuestos evade tax

evaluación *f* evaluation

evaluación de la rentabilidad
measurement of profitability

evaluar value

evaluar los costes evaluate costs

evasión *f* **de capital** flight of capital

evasión de impuestos tax avoidance;
tax evasion

examen *m* examination,
inspection, test

examinar examine, inspect

excedente *m* surplus, excess

exceder exceed

excepto excluding

excesivo(-a) excessive

exceso *m* surplus, excess

exceso de existencias overstocks

exclusiva *f* /**exclusividad** *f* exclusivity

exclusivo(-a) sole

exención *f* **fiscal** tax exemption

exento(-a) exempt (adj)

exhibición *f* display, exhibition

exhibir display, exhibit

exigir demand, claim; require

eximir exempt

existencias *fpl* inventory, stock

existencias finales closing stock

existencias iniciales opening stock

éxito *m* success

éxito, tener succeed, do well

expedición *f* consignment, shipping

expedidor(a) shipper,
forwarding agent

expediente *m* dossier, file

expedir dispatch, send, ship, forward

experimentado(-a) experienced

experto(-a) experienced

exponer exhibit, display

exportación *f* export

exportaciones exports

exportador(a) exporter

exposición *f*
exhibition, display; exposure

expositor(a) exhibitor

expropiación *f* **forzosa**
compulsory purchase

extender extend

extender un cheque write out a
cheque/check

extensión *f* telephone extension

extracto *m* **de cuentas**
bank statement

extranjero(-a) foreign

extranjero, en el abroad

extraoficial unofficial

extras *mpl* **opcionales**
optional extras

F

fábrica *f* factory

fabricante *m* manufacturer

fabricar manufacture

fácil uso, de user-friendly

facilidades de pago easy terms

factor *m* **de riesgo** downside factor

factor decisivo deciding factor

factura *f* bill, invoice

factura con el IVA VAT invoice

factura detallada itemized invoice

factura por duplicado duplicate
(of a) receipt

factura pro forma pro forma (invoice)

facturar bill, invoice

facturar el equipaje check in
(at airport)

facturas impagadas unpaid invoices

fallar

fallar fail
fallo m ruling; fault
falsificación f forgery, fake
falsificar forge
falta f shortage; default
falta de fondos lack of funds
faltar default
fama f standing
fecha f date
fecha de caducidad sell-by date;
   expiry date
fecha de entrega delivery date
fecha de vencimiento expiry date,
   maturity date
fecha inicial starting date
fecha tope/límite
   closing date, deadline
fecha, sin undated
fechador m date stamp
fechar date
feria f comercial trade fair
ferrocarril m railway/railroad
fiabilidad f reliability
fiable reliable
ficha f de ordenador computer file
ficha de registro filing card
fichero m file *(for documents)*;
   card index
fichero de ordenador computer file
fidelidad f a la marca brand loyalty
fiesta f holiday, festival
fiesta oficial/nacional public holiday,
   bank holiday
fijación f de precios
   (common) pricing
fijar fix, set
fijar los daños assess damages
fijo(-a) set (adj)
filial f subsidiary
fin m/**final** m end
finalizar finalize; end, expire
financiación f financing
financiamiento m financing
financiar finance, fund
financiero(-a) financial
finiquito m settlement *(payment)*
firma f signature; firm
firmante m/f signatory
firmar sign
firmar como testigo witness (v)
   (a document)
fletar un avión charter an aircraft
flete m freight *(carriage)*

flete aéreo air freight
flojo(-a) slack
floreciente flourishing
flujo m **de caja** cash flow
flujo de caja descontado discounted
   cash flow
folleto m **publicitario** brochure,
   leaflet, prospectus
fondo m fund
fondo de caja cash float
fondo de comercio goodwill
formar train, learn
formulario m form
formulario de solicitud
   application form
fórmulas fpl **judiciales** form of words
fracasado(-a) unsuccessful
fracasar fail
fracaso m failure, flop
franco(-a) free
franco a bordo free on board
franco a domicilio carriage paid
franco de porte carriage free
franco en almacén
   price ex warehouse
franco en fábrica price ex works
franquear stamp *(letter)*
franqueo m postage
franqueo concertado postage
   paid, postpaid
franqueo y embalaje postage
   and packing
franquicia f franchise
franquiciador(a) franchiser
franquiciar franchise
fraude m fraud
fraude fiscal tax evasion
frontera f border
fuente f **de ingresos** source
   of income
fuera de horas outside (office) hours
fuera de horas punta off-peak
fuerte competencia
   keen competition
fuerza f **mayor** act of God,
   force majeure
fuerzas del mercado market forces
fuga f **de capital** flight of capital
funcionar, hacer operate
funcionario(-a) official (n)
funda f cover *(top)*
fundamental fundamental, basic

fundar una compañía set up
a company
fusión f merger
fusionar merge

G

gama f range
gama de productos product line
ganancia f gain, profit, return
ganancia neta clear profit
ganancias earnings (profit)
ganar earn (money), gain
ganga f bargain (cheaper than usual)
garantía f guarantee, warranty;
collateral, cover
gastar spend (money)
gastar excesivamente overspend
gasto m expense,
outlay, expenditure
gasto de tramitación
handling charge
gastos mpl charge(s)
gastos administrativos
administrative expenses
gastos bancarios bank charges
gastos corrientes running costs,
running expenses
gastos de capital capital expenditure
gastos de carga aérea
air freight charges
gastos de descarga landing charges
gastos de explotación operating
costs, operating expenses
gastos de franqueo postal charges,
postal rates
gastos de transporte freight costs
gastos generales
overhead costs, overheads
gastos generales de fabricación
manufacturing overheads
gastos menores petty expenses,
incidental expenses
gastos no autorizados
unauthorized expenditure
general general, across-the-board
género m merchandise
gerencia f management
gerente m/f manager
gestionar negotiate
girar draw (a cheque/check)
giro m draft, remittance
giro a la vista sight draft

giro bancario bank draft
giro postal money order
gráfico m diagram
gráfico circular/sectorial pie chart
gráfico de barras bar chart
gran gasto m heavy expenditure
grandes almacenes department store
grandes costes heavy costs
granel, a loose
gratificación f por méritos merit
award, merit bonus
gratis free (of charge), gratis
gratuitamente free (of charge), gratis
gratuito(-a) free (of charge), gratis
gravamen m lien
gravar levy
gravar con un impuesto tax (v)
gruesa f gross (144)
guardar keep, store,
save (computer file)
guía f directory
guía m/f courier, guide
guía alfabética classified directory
guía comercial trade directory
guía urbana street directory

H

haber m credit balance, credit side
habilidad f ability, capacity, skill
habitación f room
hablar speak, talk
hacer negocios do business
hacer un inventario take stock
hacer un pedido order (goods)
hacerse un seguro take out a policy
herramienta f tool, implement
hipoteca f mortgage
hipotecar mortgage
hoja f de papel sheet of paper
hombre m de negocios businessman
honorarios mpl fee (for services)
hora f de apertura opening time
hora de cierre closing time
hora-hombre f man-hour
hora, por per hour
horario m timetable
horario comercial opening hours
**horario de presentación en el
aeropuerto** check-in time
horas de mayor afluencia rush hour
horas de oficina business hours
horas extraordinarias overtime

horas punta

horas punta peak period, rush hour
hueco *m* **de un mercado** niche, gap in the market
huelga *f* strike
huelguista *m/f* striker
hundimiento *m* collapse
hundirse collapse
hurto *m* **en las tiendas** shoplifting

I

I+D R&D (research and development)
idóneo(-a) suitable
ilegalmente illegally
imagen *f* **pública de una empresa** corporate image
imitación *f* fake
impago *m* non-payment *(of a debt)*
importaciones *fpl* imports
importador(a) importer
importar matter; import
importe *m* amount *(of money)*
importe debido amount owing
importe pagado amount paid
imposible de conseguir unobtainable
imposición *f* bank deposit; taxation
imposición a plazo time deposit
imposición indirecta indirect taxation
impositor(a) depositor
impresión *f* printout
impreso *m* form
impreso de solicitud application form
impresora *f* printer *(machine)*
imprevistos *mpl* incidental expenses
imprimir print out
impuesto *m* tax
impuesto atrasado back tax
impuesto de sociedades corporation tax
impuesto de venta purchase tax
impuesto del timbre stamp duty
impuesto no incluido exclusive of tax
impuesto pagado tax paid
impuesto progresivo graduated tax, progressive tax
impuesto sobre el consumo excise duty
impuesto sobre el valor añadido value added tax (VAT)
impuesto sobre la renta income tax
impuesto sobre la venta sales tax
impuestos incluidos inclusive of tax

impuestos retenidos en el origen tax deducted at source
inalcanzable unobtainable
inasequible unavailable
incautación *f* seizure
incautar seize
incluir include
incompetencia *f* inefficiency
incompetente inefficient
incorporado(-a) built-in
incrementar increase
incremento *m* increase
incumplimiento *m* default, breach of contract
incumplir default
incumplir los pagos default on payments
incurrir incur *(costs)*
indemnidad *f* indemnity
indemnización *f* indemnification, compensation
indemnizar indemnify, compensate
indicar mark, point out, specify
índice *m* index; rate
índice de precios al consumo consumer price index
índice ponderado weighted index
indiciación *f* indexation
industria principal staple industry
industria próspera/en expansión boom industry
industrial *m/f* industrialist
ineficacia *f* inefficiency
ineficaz inefficient
inflacionario(-a)/inflacionista inflationary
influir influence
información privilegiada insider dealing
informar inform, report (v)
informatizar computerize
informe *m* report
informe anual annual report
infraestructura *f* infrastructure
infringir la ley break the law
ingeniero(-a) de obra site engineer
ingresar deposit
ingresar en join
ingreso *m* entry, admission; bank deposit
ingreso real real income
ingresos *mpl* earnings, revenue, income, receipts

ingresos de un negocio takings
ingresos invisibles
  invisible earnings
iniciales a, poner las initial (v)
iniciar conversaciones
  initiate discussions
iniciativa, tomar la take the initiative
inmovilizar capital lock up capital
inquietud f concern, worry
inquilino(-a) lessee, tenant, occupier
inscribir write in, enrol
inscribir en un registro register
  (in official list)
inscripción f registration
insolvencia f bankruptcy
insolvente bankrupt, insolvent
inspección f examination, inspection
inspeccionar inspect
inspector(a) de Hacienda
  tax inspector
inspector(a) de obra surveyor
instalaciones fpl facilities
instrucciones fpl instructions,
  directions for use
instrucciones de envío
  forwarding instructions
instrucciones, dar issue instructions
instrumento m instrument,
  tool, implement
intercambiar exchange, swap
intercambio m exchange, swap
interés m interest (paid
  on investment)
interés compuesto
  compound interest
interés elevado high interest
interés personal/intereses creados
  vested interest
interesar interest, appeal to
intermediario(-a)
  intermediary, middleman
interno(-a) internal, in-house
interrumpir interrupt, discontinue
intervenir una cuenta audit
  an account
interventor(a) auditor
introducir datos input information
introducir gradualmente phase in
invalidar invalidate, void
invariable invariable, constant
inventario m inventory,
  stock list; stocktaking
inversión f investment

inversión segura safe investment
inversor(a) investor
invertido(-a) invested
invertir invest
investigación f
  investigation, research
investigación de mercado
  market research
investigación sobre el consumo
  consumer research
investigación y desarrollo research
  and development
investigador(a) researcher
investigar investigate, research
IVA VAT (value added tax)
izquierdo(-a) left (not right)

J

jefe(-a) boss (informal)
jefe(-a) de departamento
  head of department
jefe(-a) de distribución
  distribution manager
jefe(-a) de equipo de ventas field
  sales manager
jefe(-a) de personal
  personnel manager
jefe(-a) ejecutivo(-a) chief executive
jornada f working day
jornada completa, a full-time
jornal m wage
jubilarse retire (from one's job)
judicial judicial, legal
juicio m lawsuit
junta f meeting
junta directiva/de directores board
  of directors, management
junta general anual annual general
  meeting (AGM)
juntar join
jurídico(-a) legal
justificar justify, account for
justo(-a) fair, honest
juzgado m court, tribunal

L

lanzamiento m launch,
  launching; flotation
largo(-a) long
largo plazo long-term
letra f bill, draft

letra a largo plazo long-dated bill
letra al propio cargo promissory note
letra de cambio bill of exchange
letras a cobrar bills receivable
letras a pagar bills payable
letrero *m* sign
levantar un embargo lift an embargo
levantar una sesión close a meeting
ley *f* law
ley de prescripción statute of limitations
libra *f* pound
libra esterlina pound sterling
librado(-a) drawee
librador(a) drawer
libramiento *m* money order, bank mandate
libre free, vacant
libre de impuestos duty-free, tax-free
libro *m* **de caja** cash book
libro diario journal *(accounts book)*
libro mayor ledger
libro mayor de compras bought ledger
licencia *f* licence/license, permit
licencia de exportación export licence/license, export permit
licencia de importación import licence/license, import permit
licencia por maternidad maternity leave
licenciado(-a) en prácticas graduate trainee
líder *m* leader
limitar limit, restrict
límite *m* limit; deadline
límite de crédito credit limit, lending limit
límite de precios price ceiling
línea *f* telephone line
línea de productos product line
línea ocupada engaged *(telephone)*
liquidación *f* liquidation, sale
liquidación de inventario stock-taking sale
liquidar liquidate, realize
liquidar existencias clear stock
liquidar propiedades realize property
liquidar una compañía wind up a company
liquidar una cuenta settle an account
liquidez *f* liquidity

lista *f* **de contenidos** packing list, packing slip
lista de correos poste restante
lista de destinatarios mailing list
lista de direcciones address list
lista de existencias stock list
lista de precios fija fixed scale of charges
lista negra, poner en la blacklist (v)
listo(-a) ready; clever
llamada *f* phone call
llamada a cobro revertido reverse charge call, collect call
llamada de fuera incoming call
llamar call, phone, telephone
llamar a cobro revertido reverse the charges, call collect
llegadas *fpl* arrivals
llegar arrive
llegar a un acuerdo reach an agreement
llenar un vacío fill a gap
lleno(-a) full
llevar ante los tribunales take (so.) to court
llevar direct, run, manage; take, carry *(transport)*
llevar negociaciones conduct negotiations
llevar un negocio carry on a business
local *m* premises
local comercial business premises
local de exposición stand *(at exhibition)*
logotipo *m* logo
lonja *f* exchange, market
lote *m* batch *(of products)*
lucrativo(-a) profitable
lugar *m* place, site
lugar de trabajo place of work
lugar, tener take place

M

magistratura *f* **del trabajo** industrial tribunal
mala calidad *f* poor quality
malentendido *m* misunderstanding
maletas *fpl* luggage, baggage
maletín *m* briefcase
malgastar waste

mandamiento *m* writ
mandante *m* principal *(person)*
mandar por correo post, mail (v)
mandato *m* writ
mando *m* control, power
mandos *mpl* **intermedios**
middle management
mano *f* **de obra** manpower
mano de obra barata cheap
labour/labor
mano de obra cualificada skilled
labour/labor
mantener maintain, keep up
mantenimiento *m* maintenance
manual de funcionamiento
operating manual
manual de mantenimiento
service manual
maqueta *f* mock-up, model
máquina *f* **franqueadora**
franking machine
máquina, pasar a keyboard, type
maquinaria *f* machinery,
plant, equipment
maquinista *m/f* machinist, operator
marca *f* mark; brand, make
marca comercial brand name,
trademark, trade name
marca registrada
registered trademark
marcador *m* marker pen
marcar mark
marcar un número dial a number
marco *m* mark, Deutschmark
margen *m* margin, profit
margen de beneficio mark-up,
profit margin
más o menos more or less
material *m* **de embalaje**
packaging material
material de exposición
display material
materias *fpl* **primas** raw materials
matrícula *f* registration (fee);
number plate
matriz *f* counterfoil
máximo *m* **autorizado** ceiling price
mayor, al por wholesale
mayoría *f* majority
mayorista *m/f* wholesaler
mechera *f* shoplifter
media *f* mean, average
mediador(a) mediator

mediador de conflictos
problem solver
mediano(-a) average, medium-sized
medición *f* **de la rentabilidad**
measurement of profitability
medidas, tomar take action
medidas *fpl* **de precaución**
safety precautions
medidas fiscales fiscal measures
medio(-a) half; average (adj)
medios *mpl* means; facilities
medios de comunicación media
medios fraudulentos false pretences
mejorar improve, recover
mejoría *f* improvement, recovery
memoria *f* report; computer memory
mencionar mention, refer to *(item)*
mensaje *m* message
mensajero(-a) courier *(messenger)*
mensual monthly (adj)
mercadeo *m*
marketing, merchandizing
mercader *m* merchant
mercado *m* market
mercado a futuros forward market
mercado cautivo captive market
mercado cerrado closed market
mercado de valores stock market
mercado interior/nacional
domestic market
mercado libre open market,
free market
mercado negro black market
mercado previsto target market;
market forecast
mercados exteriores
overseas markets
mercadotecnia *f* marketing
mercancía *f* commodity
mercancía exportada export
mercancías *fpl* goods, merchandise
mercancías a precio reducido
cut-price goods
mercancías perecederas
perishable goods
mes *m* month
mes civil calendar month
mesa *f* **de despacho** desk
minoría *f* minority
minorista *m/f* retailer
mitad *f* half
moda, pasado(-a) de old-fashioned
modelo *m* model; standard

modelo a escala model, mock-up
modelo de prueba
  demonstration model
modernizar modernize, update
moderno(-a) modern, up to date
modo *m* **de empleo** instructions
  for use
modo de pago mode of payment
moneda *f* currency; coin
moneda convertible/fuerte
  convertible/hard currency
moneda extranjera foreign currency
moneda no convertible soft currency
moroso(-a) defaulter; slow payer
mostrador *m* counter
mostrador de facturación
  check-in counter
mostrar demonstrate, show
mostrar un beneficio show a profit
movilizar capital mobilize capital
muelle *m* quay
muestra *f* sample, trial sample
muestra aleatoria random sample
muestra de inspección check sample
muestra gratuita free sample
muestra pequeña swatch
muestreo *m* **de aceptación**
  acceptance sampling
muestreo por áreas
  sampling, testing
mujer *f* **de negocios**
  business-woman
multa *f* fine
multar fine
mundial worldwide
mundo *m* world
muy bien pagado(-a) highly-paid
muy caro(-a) highly-priced
muy moderno(-a) state-of-the-art

N

nacional, de ámbito nationwide
nada *f* nothing, nil
necesidades *fpl* requirements
negar refuse
negativa *f* refusal
negociaciones *f* **salariales**
  wage negotiations
negociador(a) negotiator
negociante *m/f* merchant
negociar negotiate; trade; bargain
negocio *m* bargain, deal; business

negocio descuidado
  neglected business
negocio suplementario sideline
negocios *mpl* business,
  commerce, trade
neto(-a) net (adj)
nivel *m* level
nivelarse level off, level out
nombrar appoint
nombrar por coopción co-opt so.
nombre *m* **comercial** trademark,
  trade name, brand name
nombre de, en on behalf of
norma *f* standard; rule
normal normal, standard;
  regular, ordinary
normalizar standardize
normas regulations
normas de conducta code of practice
nota *f* note, memo
nota de abono/de crédito credit note
nota de adeudo debit note
nota de aviso advice note
nota de cobertura cover note
nota de depósito deposit slip,
  paying-in slip
nota de expedición/de envío
  consignment note, dispatch note
nota, tomar note, minute (v)
notable outstanding, exceptional
notario *m* notary public
notificar notify
nuevo pedido reorder
numerar number
número *m* number
número de serie serial number
números numbers, statistics
números impares odd numbers

O

obedecer obey, comply with
objetivo(-a) objective (adj)
objetivo *m* objective, aim
objetivo de producción
  production target
objetivo de ventas sales target
objeto *m* **de una OPA** takeover target
obligación *f*
  obligation, duty; debenture
obligación perpetua
  irredeemable bond

obligaciones *fpl* liabilities
obligaciones a corto plazo
current liabilities
obligatorio(-a) compulsory
obrar operate
obrero(-a) manual worker
obsequio *m* present, gift
obsequio publicitario
premium offer
obtener obtain
obtener beneficios brutos
gross (v)
obtener el título de qualify as
ocupación *f*
occupation, employment
ocupado(-a) busy, in use
ocupar un vacío fill a gap
ocuparse de attend to, deal with
ocurrir occur, happen
oferta *f* bid; offer; supply
oferta de lanzamiento
introductory offer
oferta en metálico cash offer
oferta especial special offer
oferta monetaria money supply
oferta pública de adquisición
takeover bid
ofertas de trabajo appointments
vacant, situations vacant
ofertas lacradas/cerradas
sealed tenders
oficial official, formal
oficial, no unofficial
oficina *f* **central** head office
oficina central de correos general
post offfice
oficina de información
information bureau
oficina de reclamaciones
complaints department
oficina principal main office,
head office
oficinas de alquiler offices to let
oficinista *m/f* clerk
oficioso(-a) unofficial
ofrecer offer *(to buy)*
opción *f* **de compra** option
to purchase
operación *f* **llaves en mano**
turnkey operation
operador(a) de teclado keyboarder
operario(-a) operator
optar decide on *(a course of action)*

orden *f* order, instruction;
writ, warrant
orden de domiciliación
banker's order
orden de pago money order
orden del día agenda
ordenador *m* computer
ordenador personal
personal computer
ordinario ordinary, regular
organigrama *m* flow chart;
organization chart
organizar organize, arrange
origen *m* origin
oscilación *f* fluctuation
oscilar fluctuate

P

pactar covenant, contract
pacto *m* pact, covenant
padrino *m* sponsor
paga *f* pay, salary, wage
paga extraordinaria de Navidad
Christmas bonus
pagadero(-a) payable
pagadero a la entrega payable
on delivery
pagadero a la vista payable
on demand
pagadero por adelantado payable
in advance
pagado(-a) paid *(invoice)*
pagado(-a) por adelantado prepaid
pagador(a) payer
pagar pay; pay out; repay
pagar al contado/en efectivo
pay cash
pagar por adelantado
pay in advance
pagar una factura settle an invoice
pagar, a overdue
pagaré *m* debenture; IOU,
promissory note
pago *m* payment, settlement
pago a cuenta interim payment,
payment on account
pago al contado payment in cash,
cash payment
pago anticipado advance payment
pago en metálico/en efectivo
payment in cash
pago inicial down payment

pago mediante cheque

pago mediante cheque payment by cheque/check
pago por adelantado prepayment; money up front
pago simbólico token payment
pago único lump sum
pagos por etapas staged payments
país *m* **de origen** country of origin
pantalla *f* monitor, screen
papeleo *m* paperwork; red tape
paquete *m* pack, parcel
parado(-a) unemployed
paraíso *m* **fiscal** tax haven
parar stop *(doing sth.)*
paro *m* unemployment
paro, en unemployed
parte *f* party; proportion
parte de baja doctor's certificate
parte demandada defendant
pasaje *m* fare
pasante *m/f* junior clerk
pasar spend *(time)*
pasar a cuenta nueva carry forward
pasarse a switch over to
pasivo *m* liabilities
pasivo circulante current liabilities
patente *f* patent
patente en tramitación patent pending
patente solicitada patent applied for
patrocinador(a) sponsor
patrocinar sponsor
patrocinio *m* sponsorship
patrón(a) boss, employer
patrón *m* standard
peaje *m* toll
pedido(-a) on order
pedido *m* order *(for goods)*
pedido cursado al viajante journey order
pedido no servido unfulfilled order
pedido por correo mail-order
pedido suplementario repeat order
pedido urgente rush order
pedidos pendientes back orders, outstanding orders
pedidos por servir dues *(orders)*
pedir ask, request; inquire
pedir más detalles ask for further details/particulars
peligroso(-a) dangerous
pendiente pending; outstanding, unpaid

pequeñas empresas *fpl* small businesses
pequeño hurto *m*/**robo** *m* pilferage, pilfering
perder miss *(train, plane)*
perder dinero lose money
perder un depósito forfeit a deposit
perder un pedido lose an order
perder valor depreciate, lose value
pérdida *f* loss; damage; wastage
pérdida de ejercicio trading loss
pérdida de valor depreciation, loss of value
pérdida sobre el papel paper loss
pérdida total total loss, write-off
periodo *m* **de espera** waiting time
periodo de prueba trial period, probation period
permiso *m* permit, permission, licence/license
permiso de exportación export licence/license, export permit
permiso de trabajo work permit
permitir permit
perseguir chase, follow up
personal *m* personnel
personal administrativo administrative staff
personal de ventas sales people
personal eventual temporary staff
personal reducido al mínimo skeleton staff
personal, asignar man (v)
personal, reclutar recruit new staff
personalidad *f* **jurídica** legal status
perspectivas *fpl* prospects
pesar weigh
peseta *f* peseta
peso *m* weight; peso *(South American currency)*
peso bruto gross weight
peso neto net weight
petición *f* request
petición de informes inquiry
petición de informes sobre crédito status inquiry
petición, a on request
petróleo *m* oil *(petroleum)*
PIB GDP (gross domestic product)
pieza *f* **de recambio** spare part
piso *m* floor *(level)*; flat/apartment
plan *m* plan, project

plan de emergencia contingency plan

plan de trabajo de una empresa corporate plan

plan, hacer un plan (v)

planear plan

planificación *f* **a largo plazo** long-term planning

planificar plan

plano *m* plan *(drawing)*

planta *f* floor plan

plaza *f* position, job; place, seat

plazo *m* period; term *(of validity)*; deadline; instalment

plazo de entrega delivery time

plazo medio medium-term

plazo, a corto on a short-term basis

pleito *m* lawsuit

plusvalía *f* capital gains

PNB GNP (gross national product)

poder *m* **adquisitivo** purchasing power

poder notarial, poderes *mpl* power of attorney

poderhabiente *m/f* proxy

política *f* politics, policy

política de precios pricing policy

póliza *f* **de seguros** insurance policy

póliza a todo riesgo all-risks policy

póliza provisional cover note

poner en práctica implement, put into practice

poner por escrito put in writing

porcentaje *m* **de comisión** cost plus

porcentaje de descuento percentage discount

porcentaje fijo flat rate

pormenores *mpl* particulars

portador(a) bearer; payee

portátil portable

porte *m* freight, carriage

porte debido freight forward, carriage forward

porte pagado carriage paid; postpaid

poseer possess

posible comprador(a) prospective buyer

posición *f* status

posponer postpone, hold over

postura *f* **negociadora** bargaining position

precauciones *fpl* safety precautions

precintar seal *(attach a seal)*

precio *m* price, tariff, rate; charge

precio a destajo piece rate

precio acordado/convenido agreed price

precio al cierre closing price

precio al contado cash price

precio al por mayor trade price

precio al por menor retail price

precio con descuento discount price

precio con entrega de artículo usado trade-in price

precio de catálogo catalogue/catalog price, list price

precio de conversión conversion price, conversion rate

precio de coste cost price

precio de entrada admission charge

precio de entrega delivered price

precio de entrega inmediata spot price

precio de/en fábrica factory price, price ex works

precio de oferta supply price

precio de subvención support price

precio en firme firm price

precio excesivo overcharge (n)

precio facturado invoice price, invoice value

precio fijo set price

precio justo fair price

precio medio/corriente average price

precio por unidad unit price

precio puesto en almacén price ex warehouse

precio reducido cut price, reduced rate

precio simbólico token charge

precio sin descuento full price

precio todo incluido all-in price, inclusive charge

precio tope ceiling price

precio umbral threshold price

precio vigente going rate

precio a, poner price (v)

precios reventados rock-bottom prices

precisar specify

predecir forecast

preempaquetar prepack, prepackage

prefijo *m* dialling code

preguntar ask, inquire *(information)*

preocupación *f* concern, worry

preparación de pedidos

preparación f **de pedidos**
order processing
preparado(-a) ready
preparar train, teach;
prepare, process
preparar un contrato draw up
a contract
preparar una factura raise an invoice
prepararse train, learn
prescribir lapse
preselección f shortlist
preseleccionar shortlist
presentar present, show,
submit; introduce
presentar una cuenta/una factura
render an account
presentar una letra a la aceptación
present a bill for acceptance
presentar una reconvención
counter-claim (v)
presentarse attend, report; check in
(at airport)
presentarse a una entrevista report
for an interview
presente present (adj)
(being there)
presidente(-a) chairman
(of company)
presidente y director gerente
chairman and managing director
prestado, pedir/tomar borrow
prestamista m/f lender
préstamo m loan
préstamo a plazo fijo term loan
préstamo garantizado secured loan
prestar lend
prestar atención take notice,
attend to
prestatario(-a) debtor, borrower
presupuestar budget
presupuesto m budget
presupuesto estimate,
quote, quotation
presupuesto de promoción
promotional budget
presupuesto de ventas sales budget
presupuesto provisional
provisional budget
presupuesto publicitario
advertising budget
prevención f prevention
prever forecast
previsión f forecast

previsión de mano de obra
manpower forecasting
prima f bonus
prima de seguros
insurance premium
prima por ausencia de siniestralidad
no-claims bonus
primeras entradas, primeras salidas
first in first out
principal principal, chief (adj)
principal m principal (money)
principio m principle
probar test
proceso m **judicial** lawsuit,
legal proceedings
procurador(a) lawyer, attorney
producción f **en serie/a gran escala**
mass production
producción interior/nacional
domestic production
productivo(-a)
productive, profitable
producto m product, commodity
producto defectuoso reject
producto ficticio dummy
producto final end product
Producto Interior Bruto gross
domestic product (GDP)
Producto Nacional Bruto gross
national product (GNP)
productos de marca propia own
label goods
productos devueltos sin vender
returns (unsold goods)
productos en competencia
competing products
profesional m/f professional
programa m programme/program,
timetable; agenda
programa de ordenador
computer program
programa informático software
programa piloto pilot scheme
programar plan, timetable;
program (computer)
prohibición f ban, embargo
prohibir ban, embargo
prolongación f extension
prolongar extend
promedio m mean
promesa f promise, undertaking
promoción f promotion, publicity
promocionar promote, advertise

pronosticar forecast
pronóstico m forecast
pronto pago m prompt payment
propiedad f ownership
propiedad inmobiliaria real estate
propiedad privada private property
propietario(-a) landlord, proprietor, owner
propietario(-a) legítimo(-a) rightful owner
propietario(-a) único(-a) sole owner
propina f tip *(money)*
proponerse aim, propose *(to do sth.)*
propósito m aim
prorrata, a pro rata
prórroga f extension
prórroga de un arrendamiento renewal of a lease
prorrogar extend
proseguir continue
prospecto m prospectus
prosperar succeed, do well
próspero(-a) flourishing, successful
proteger safeguard
prototipo m **de contrato** model agreement
proveedor(a) supplier
proveer supply
próximo(-a) next, close to
proyectar plan, design
proyecto m project, draft, rough plan
prueba f test
prueba, a on approval
publicar publish, release, make public
publicidad f publicity
publicidad en el punto de venta point of sale material
publicidad por correo direct-mail advertising; mail shot
publicidad, dar publicize
puerta en puerta, de door-to-door
puerto m port, harbour/harbor
puerto de embarque port of embarkation
puerto de escala port of call
puesto m post, position, job
puesto aduanero customs entry point
puesto clave key post
punto m point, item on agenda
punto de referencia benchmark
punto de venta point of sale

punto decimal decimal point
punto muerto breakeven point; deadlock

Q

quebrado m bankrupt
quebrado no rehabilitado undischarged bankrupt
quebrar fail
quedar remain *(be left)*
quedarse atrás fall behind *(worse position)*
queja f complaint
quejarse complain *(about)*
querellante m/f plaintiff
quiebra f bankruptcy
quitar take off

R

rama f branch, division *(of company)*
rápido(-a) express, fast
ratero(-a) de tiendas shoplifter
razón f reason; ratio
razón social trade name
reacción f reaction, response
reactivación f recovery, getting better
reajuste m adjustment
realización f realization, implementation
reanudar las negociaciones resume negotiations
rebaja f reduction, cut
rebajar reduce, cut, mark down, take off
rebajas fpl sale *(at low price)*
rebajas de fin de temporada end of season sale
recado m message
recargar mark up, increase
recargo m surcharge
recaudación f **de impuestos** tax collection, levy
recaudador(a) collector
recaudar levy
recepción f reception, receiving; reception desk
rechazar reject, turn down; refuse
rechazo m rejection, refusal
recibir receive; take *(a call)*
recibo m receipt *(piece of paper)*

recibo de depósito

recibo de depósito paying-in slip
reciclar recycle; retrain
recipiente m container
reclamación f claim; request, demand for payment
reclamar demand, claim
recobrar recover
recoger collect (fetch)
recogida f collection (of goods)
reconocer a un sindicato recognize a union
reconvención f counter-claim
recortar cut, reduce
recorte m cut
recuperación f recovery, retrieval
recuperar recover, retrieve
recursos mpl resources, means
redactar un contrato draft/draw up a contract
redimir redeem
redondear por defecto round down
redondear por exceso round up
reducción f decrease, reduction
reducir decrease, reduce
reducir drásticamente slash (prices, credit terms)
reducir gastos cut down on expenses
reducir gradualmente phase out
reembolsable repayable
reembolsar refund, repay
reembolso m refund
reemplazo m replacement (item)
reembolsable repayable
referente relating to
referirse concern, refer to, apply to
refrendar countersign
regalar give, give away (as gift)
regalo m gift, present
regargo m overcharge
regatear bargain
regir be in force
registrar examine; record, register (in official list)
registrarse check in (at hotel)
registro m register; registry; entry; examination, inspection; registration
Registro Mercantil Registrar of Companies
regla f rule
reglamentar regulate (by law)
reglamento m rule, regulations

regreso m return, going back
regular regular (at same time)
rehusar refuse
reinversión f reinvestment
reinvertir reinvest
reivindicar claim (insurance)
relación f index; ratio; connection
relación precio-ganancias price/earnings ratio (P/E ratio)
relaciones fpl **laborales** industrial relations
relaciones públicas public relations (PR)
relativo a relating to, regarding
rellenar fill a gap
rematar knock down (a price)
remate m distress sale
remesa f consignment (things sent)
remite m return address
remitente m/f sender; return address
remitir refer (pass to so.)
remitir adjunto enclose
remitir por cheque remit by cheque/check
rendimiento m return, profit, yield; production capacity; output, throughput, goods
rendimiento de la inversión return on investment
rendimiento efectivo effective yield
rendimiento neto net yield
rendir yield, bear
rendir cuentas a alguien report to so.
renovación f renewal
renovar renew
renovar existencias restock
renovar un pedido reorder, repeat an order
renta f income; rent
renta de inversiones investment income
renta fija fixed income
renta imponible taxable income
rentabilidad f profitability, cost-effectiveness
rentabilidad del dividendo dividend yield
rentable profitable, cost-effective
renuncia f disclaimer
renunciar renounce, waive
repartir distribute; divide among, share; deliver
repartir un riesgo spread a risk

reparto m distribution
repertorio m trade directory
repostar restock
representante m/f agent; representative, salesman
representante en exclusiva sole agent
repuesto m replacement; spare part
reputación f standing
requerimiento de pago demand (for payment)
requisitos mpl requirements
resarcir compensate, make good (a loss)
rescatar save, rescue
rescate m recovery; redemption (of a loan); salvage, rescue; surrender (of insurance)
rescindir un contrato cancel a contract
reserva f reservation; reserve (of money)
reserva anticipada advance booking
reserva en bloque block booking
reserva en dólares dollar balance
reservar book
reservar con exceso overbook
reservas fpl reserve(s)
reservas ocultas hidden reserves
resguardo m slip, receipt
residuos mpl waste
resignar resign
respaldar back up, support
responder answer, reply
responder de account for
responsabilidad f responsibility
responsabilidad contractual contractual liability
responsabilidad limitada limited liability
responsable responsible (for)
responsable de liable for
respuesta f answer, reply; response
resto m remainder (things left)
restringir restrict
resultados mpl figures, results
retirar withdraw (money, offer)
retirar gradualmente phase out
retirarse retire (from one's job)
retrasar hold up, delay
retrasarse fall behind (be late)
retraso m hold-up, delay

retraso, con late (adv)
reunión f meeting
reunión de personal staff meeting
reunión de ventas sales conference
reunirse meet (so.)
revaluar reassess, revalue
revelación f disclosure
reventa f resale
revertido(-a) reverse (adj)
revés m setback
revisar examine, inspect; service (a machine)
revisar las cuentas audit the accounts
revisión f service (of machine)
revisión de cuentas audit
revisión de sueldos salary review
revista f magazine
revocar revoke, countermand
riesgo m risk
robo m theft
robo en las tiendas shoplifting
romper break off (negotiations); break (agreement)
rotulador m marker pen
rótulo m sign
rubricar initial
ruego m request

S

S.A. Ltd (limited company), Inc.
S.R.L. Ltd (limited company)
sacar withdraw (money)
sacar el título de qualify as
sala f de embarque departure lounge
sala de juntas/de conferencias conference room
salario m pay, salary
salario interesante attractive salary
salario mínimo minimum wage
salarios reales real wages
saldar balance
saldo m balance
saldo sale (at low price)
saldo a cuenta nueva balance carried down/carried forward
saldo acreedor/a favor credit balance
saldo de caja cash balance
saldo de cuenta bancaria bank balance

saldo deudor

saldo deudor/a favor balance due to us
saldo final closing balance
saldo inicial opening balance
salidas *fpl* departures
saltarse la cola jump the queue/line
salvamento *m* salvage
salvar salvage, rescue
salvedad *f* proviso
salvo error u omisión errors and omissions excepted
sancionar penalize
satisfacer una demanda satisfy/meet a demand
saturar el mercado saturate the market
sección *f* department; division *(part of a company)*
sección de compras buying department
sección de ventas sales department
secretario(-a) eventual temp
secretario(-a) personal personal assistant (PA)
sector *m* **primario** primary industry
sector privado private sector
sector público public sector
secuestrar seize
secuestro *m* seizure
secundario(-a) subsidiary, secondary
sede *f* headquarters
según according to
según contrato contractually
según factura as per invoice
según muestra as per sample
según nota de expedición as per advice
segunda mano, de secondhand
seguridad *f* **de empleo** security of employment
seguridad en el empleo job security
seguro *m* insurance; life assurance
seguro a todo riesgo comprehensive insurance
seguro corriente de vida whole-life insurance
seguro de la vivienda house insurance
sellar seal *(attach a seal)*
sello *m* postage stamp
semana, por per week
semanalmente weekly

semestre *m* half-year
señal *f* deposit *(in advance)*; sign; mark
señal de comunicar engaged tone
señal de línea dialling tone
señalar mark, point out
señas *fpl* address
servicio *m* service *(dealing with customers)*
servicio de atención al cliente customer service department
servicio de contestación answering service
servicio de mantenimiento service department
servicio deficiente poor service
servicio posventa after-sales/customer service
servicio rápido prompt service
servicios de informática computer services
servir un pedido deal with an order
signatario(-a) colectivo(-a) joint signatory
sindicalista *m/f* trade unionist
sindicato *m* trade union
síndico *m* receiver, liquidator
siniestro *m* loss
sistema *m* **informático** computer system
sitio *m* site, place
situación *f* situation, state of affairs
sobornar bribe
soborno *m* bribe
sobrar remain
sobrecapacidad *f* overcapacity
sobrecontratación *m* overbooking
sobregiro *m* overdraft
sobrepasar exceed
sobreprima *f* additional premium
sobreproducción *f* overproduction
sobresaliente outstanding, exceptional
sobretasa *f* surcharge
sociedad *f* company
sociedad anónima public limited company/corporation
sociedad de cartera holding company
sociedad limitada limited (liability) company
sociedad matriz parent company
sociedad mercantil corporation

socio(-a) associate, partner
socio comanditario/en comandita sleeping partner
solar m site
solicitar request
solicitar pedidos solicit orders
solicitar un trabajo apply for a job
solicitud f application, request
someter a prueba test
sondeo m **de opinión** opinion poll
sostener maintain, support
subarrendar sublease, sublet
subarriendo m sublease
subasta f auction
subastar auction
subcontratar subcontract
subcontratista m/f subcontractor
subcontrato m subcontract
subdirector(a) assistant manager
subida f rise, increase
subida en precio/en valor increase, appreciation *(in value)*
subir increase, raise *(price)*, rise
subsidio de carestía de vida cost-of-living allowance
subvención f subsidy
subvencionar subsidize
sucursal f branch
sueldo m wage, salary
sueldo bruto gross salary
sueldo neto net salary
suelto(-a) loose
sufragar defray *(costs)*
sujeto(-a) a subject to, liable to
suma f **global** lump sum
suma total grand total
sumar total
suministrador(a) supplier
suministro m supply
suministrar supply
superar exceed
superávit m surplus
superficie f **útil** floor space
supervisión, de supervisory
supervisor(a) supervisor
suplemento m endorsement *(on insurance)*
suplemento por el servicio service charge
suplente m/f deputy
suprimir delete
surtido m choice *(items to choose from)*

suspender suspend, discontinue, cancel
suspender pagos stop payments
suspendido(-a) cancelled
suspensión f **de pagos** suspension of payments
sustituir a alguien deputize for/ replace so.

T

tablero m **de hojas sueltas** flip chart
talla f **corriente** stock size
talla muy grande outsize
talonario m **de cheques** cheque/check book
tamaño m **corriente** stock size
tanto m **alzado** flat rate
tanto por ciento percentage
taquillero(-a) booking clerk
tara f defect
tarde late (adv)
tarea f job, task
tarifa f tariff, price, rate
tarifa de horas extras overtime pay
tarifa horaria hourly rate
tarifa postal postage
tarifa reducida reduced/cheap rate
tarifas publicitarias advertising rates
tarjeta f card *(business card)*
tarjeta de cajero automático cash card
tarjeta de crédito credit card
tarjeta de embarque boarding card/pass
tarjeta oro gold card
tasa f rate
tasa f **de interés** interest rate
tasa de cambio exchange rate
tasa de crecimiento growth rate
tasa de impuestos normal standard rate (of tax)
tasación f valuation
tasar value
tecla f key *(on keyboard)*
teclado m **numérico** numeric keypad
teclear keyboard
telefonear telephone, phone
teléfono m **de tarjeta** card phone
teléfono móvil mobile phone
teléfono público pay phone
temporada f **baja** off-season

tendencias del mercado

tendencias *fpl* **del mercado**
market trends

tenencia *f* **de acciones**
shareholding

tener en existencia carry, have
in stock

tercero *m* third party

terminal *m* **de ordenador**
computer terminal

terminar terminate, end, finish

terminar de trabajar stop work

términos *mpl* terms

terna *f* shortlist

testigo *m/f*/**testimonio** *m* witness

tiempo, a on time

tiempo completo, a tiempo full-time

tienda *f* shop/store

tienda libre de impuestos duty-
free shop/store

tierra *f* land

tipo *m* **base de interés bancario** bank
base rate

tipo de cambio exchange rate, rate
of exchange

tipo de cambio actual current rate
of exchange

tipo de interés interest rate

tipo impositivo tax rate

título *m* deed

título al portador bearer bond

título de una acción
share/stock certificate

títulos *mpl* equities, securities

títulos del Estado government bonds

títulos profesionales
professional qualifications

tomar posesión take over *(from so.)*

tonelada *f* ton

tonelaje *m* tonnage

total *m* **acumulado** running total

total parcial subtotal

totalizar total (v)

trabajador(a) worker

trabajadores por horas
hourly-paid workers

trabajar work

trabajo *m* work; job *(piece of work)*

trabajo a destajo piecework

trabajo en curso work in progress

trabajo eventual casual work

trabajo por horas part-time work

trabajo por turnos shift work

trabajo rutinario routine work

trabajo, sin out of work

traducción *f* translation

traducir translate

traductor(a) translator

tramitar process

tramitar el pago de un cheque clear
a cheque/check

transacción *f* **global** package deal

transbordo *m* transfer

transferencia *f* **bancaria** bank
transfer

transigir compromise

transportar carry, transport

transporte *m* transport;
carriage, freight

transporte por carretera
road transport

transportista *m/f* shipper, carrier

traslado *m* transfer

tratamiento *m* **de textos**
word-processing

tratante *m* dealer

tratar attempt, try

tratar en deal in

trato *m* deal

tren *m* train

tribunal *m* court

tribunal de justicia
adjudication tribunal

tribunal de arbitraje
arbitration tribunal

tribunales de justicia law courts

trimestral quarterly (adj)

trimestre *m* quarter *(three months)*

triplicado, por in triplicate

trocar barter

trueque *m* barter

turno *m* shift *(team of workers)*

U

UE EU (European Union)

último(-a) latest

último requerimiento de pago
final demand

último trimestre last quarter

único(-a) sole, one-off

unilateral unilateral

Unión Europea European Union

urgente urgent; express, fast

usar use

usar y tirar, de disposable

uso *m* use; utilization

usuario *m* **final** end user
utilización *f* utilization
utilizar use

V

vacaciones *fpl* **reglamentarias** statutory holiday/vacation
vacante *adj* vacant
vacante *f* vacancy *(for job)*
vacío(-a) empty (adj)
vale *m* voucher
vale para un regalo gift voucher
valedero(-a) valid
valer cost; be worth
válido(-a), ser be in force
valor *m* **a la par** par value
valor contable book value
valor de activo asset value
valor de reposición replacement value
valor de rescate surrender value
valor declarado declared value
valor nominal face value, nominal value
valor total de factura total invoice value
valoración *f* estimate, evaluation, valuation
valoración de daños assessment of damages
valorar estimate, value
valores *mpl* securities
vencer expire, fall due
vencido(-a) due, overdue
vencimiento *m* expiry, expiration
vendedor(a) vendor, salesman, saleswoman
vender sell, market
vender a futuros sell forward
vender a precio más bajo undercut
vender al por menor retail goods
vender las existencias sobrantes dispose of excess stock
vender más barato undersell
venirse abajo fall through
venta *f* sale, selling
venta al contado cash sale
venta con tarjeta de crédito credit card sale
venta a domicilio door-to-door, house-to-house selling

venta forzosa forced sale, distress sale
venta por correo direct mail
venta, a la on sale
venta, en for sale
ventanilla *f* counter
ventas *fpl* sales
ventas bajas low sales
ventas en el mercado interior home sales
ventas nacionales domestic sales, home sales
ventas netas net sales
ventas previstas projected sales
vetar una decisión veto a decision
viajero(-a) diario(-a) commuter
viejo(-a) old
vigilancia *f* supervision
vigilante *m* security guard
vínculo *m* connection
violación *f* **de contrato** breach of contract
violación de patente infringement of patent
violar una patente infringe a patent
visado *m* visa
visado de entrada entry visa
visita *f* call, visit
visita comercial sin cita previa cold call
vitrina *f* **de exposición** display stand
volumen *m* **comercial** volume of trade
volumen de negocios volume of business
volumen de ventas turnover *(sales)*
volver a nombrar reappoint
volver a presentarse reapply
voto *m* **de calidad** casting vote
voto de gracias vote of thanks
voto por poderes proxy vote
vuelo *m* **chárter** charter flight
vuelo de correspondencia connecting flight
vuelo de larga distancia long-haul flight
vuelo regular scheduled flight
vuelta *f* change ; return

Z

zona *f* **franca** free trade zone